Honda

The T.T. Winning Years

by

Peter Kneale

&

Bill Snelling

Amulree Publications

Acknowledgments

We should like to give grateful thanks to our many friends and colleagues who have helped to make this book possible; to the many photographers and organisations who have allowed us to delve into their collections to bring together some rare and unseen pictures for this book; these include; Monica Clarke of Island Photographics, Geoff Cannell, Steve Colvin, Nick Nicholls, John Watterson and the Library of the Manx Museum.

Our thanks also to Nigel McClatchy and Steve Clarke, who provided valuable data, without which the book would have been much the poorer; and finally the photographic laboratory staff at Island Photographics who gave every assistance to ensure the quality of the pictures; Michael Fitzpatrick, Bill Milligan, and Geoff Ralston.

Peter Kneale & Bill Snelling

ISBN 1 901508 02 1
Honda - The T.T. Winning Years (softback)

Contents

In March 1954, Mr Soichiro Honda issued the following press statement from his Hamamatsu factory:

"Since Honda Motor Co. was established in 1948 we have achieved incredible progress owing to the tremendous enthusiasm of each of our employees. My childhood dream was to be a champion of motor racing with a machine built by myself. However, before becoming world champion, it is strongly required to establish a stable corporate structure, provided with precise production facilities and superior product design. From this point of view we have been concentrating on providing high quality products to meet Japanese domestic consumer demand and we have not had enough time to pour our efforts in motor cycle racing until now.....

.....Today we have accomplished a production system in which we have full confidence and the chance has come to compete. I have decided to participate in the T.T. race next year!

This aim is definitely a difficult one but we have to achieve it to test the viability of Japanese industrial technology and demonstrate it to the world. Our mission is the enlightenment of Japanese technology.

I here avow my intention that I will participate in the TT race and I proclaim with my fellow employees that I will pour all my energy and creative powers into winning."

It was to take Soichiro Honda another five years to make his debut in the Isle of Man, but the rest is history....

Just two years after their first entry into the T.T., Mike Hailwood holds the Ultra Lightweight and Lightweight trophies.

The Beginning

In 1949 there were some 40 motorcycle manufacturers in Japan - including Honda. By 1954 this number was down to just 10, and Honda had become the largest manufacturer of lightweight motorcycles in the world, but the machines were only sold in their own country.

Their founder, Soichiro Honda, a brilliant businessman decided that the 'Western World' needed to know about his beloved machines. He decided that a trip to Europe was vital to see the top motorcycle race meetings, and that of course included the Isle of Man T.T. Races. He was impressed and said that Honda would race on the Island. In 1958 a team from the company arrived in the Island, and with their top grade cameras photographed everything and every machine possible.

Naomi Taniguchi at the Manx Arms Corner, Onchan

So in 1959 the Honda affair with the T.T., which has blossomed over 40 years, began. The machines were 1958 125cc four-stroke machines, which had been built for their national 125cc series.

The 125cc race was to be held on the Clypse Course for the last time that year, and the team set up headquarters in the Nursery Hotel in Onchan. There were five riders, four of them Japanese - Naomi Taniguchi, Giichi Suzuki, Teisuke Tanaka and Junzo Suzuki. The fifth member, the team leader, was an American, Bill Hunt, who worked for the Honda Corporation of America. The honour of being the first Honda rider to practice on the Isle of Man went to Taniguchi.

In the race itself, Honda won the Manufacturers award at their first attempt - Taniguchi won a silver replica for sixth place, Giichi Suzuki a bronze for seventh place and Junzo Suzuki finished 11th. Tanaka also won a bronze replica for eighth place - but Bill Hunt crashed out of the race on the second lap.

Honda had arrived.

The all-conquering Honda team that started the revolution. Pictured after the Ultra Lightweight 125 race, the lineup is (left to right): Junzo Suzuki (rider), Giichi Suzuki (rider), Kiyoshi Kawashima (team manager), Naomi Taniguchi (rider), Teisuke Tanaka (rider), Bill Hunt (rider and liason), Hisaichi Sekiguchi (engineer), Shunji Hirosawa (mechanic).

1960

For the 1960 T.T. races Honda had four-cylinder 250cc machines as well as the 125cc twins, and had signed up some top Commonwealth riders as well. All races were held on the Mountain course, quite an experience for the Japanese riders.

In the Lightweight race Bob Brown gave Honda their best result to date with fourth place on the four-cylinder machine, winning a silver replica, Moto Kitano finished fifth with Naomi Taniguchi finishing sixth, both taking bronze replicas for their first races on the Mountain Course. Tom Phillis had held fourth place early on in the race but retired on the fourth lap.

In the 125cc Race, Honda riders finished in sixth to 10th places, and all won silver replicas, the order was Naomi Taniguchi, Giichi Suzuki, Sadao Shimazaki, Teisuke Tanaka and Tom Phillis.

Only the fact that M.V. riders finished first, second and

The 125 of Moto Kitano receives attention from mechanics after the first practice session, 1960.

third prevented them from taking the Manufacturers award again. Another Honda rider, Moto Kitano who had held a leaderboard place for the first two laps slowed and finished 19th.

The reliability of Honda was beginning to show - it would develop at a tremendous pace as the years progressed.

Tom Phillis waits as a mechanic fettles his 250cc Honda-4 at Jurby Airfield, a favourite testing ground for race teams.

Foreword
by Joey Dunlop OBE, MBE

For Honda to be involved with a book like this came as no surprise. Having raced for Honda for so long I know what the Isle of Man TT races mean to everyone at Honda throughout the world.

To be part of Honda in 1998, its 50th anniversary year, is an honour and something that will give me and many more people long-lasting memories.

This book covers the heritage of a manufacturer at the TT - a heritage which must be the envy of many other manufacturers.

But the hard work and effort, and above all the commitment to racing, is there for all to see. From the early days of Honda at the TT through to 1998 the relationship has grown to the extent that Honda now plays a big part of the annual races.

To be offered the chance to write this foreword brings back some great memories of racing for Honda on the Island. From my early days of big Japanese involvement to present day where every year Honda seems to break new records on the Isle of Man.

Ninety-three race wins are such an achievement in a short period of time but the TT wins for Honda are also about the men, the machines and the memories that go with them.

I'm sure for road racing fans around the world the memories are wide-ranging and clear, even legendary and that is what makes the TT so special.

For that reason alone there is no wonder Honda puts so

much effort into the TT every year.

From what began as a test of reliability of machinery for most of the manufacturers, the TT has now become a great motorcycling festival and something I am proud to be part of.

With that in mind I would like to thank Honda on behalf of all the riders it has supported at the TT, not just the winners, but also those who have contributed to a great name achieving great success at a great event.

Honda - The T.T. Winning Years 9

Mike Hailwood has the advantage over Luigi Taveri at Governors Bridge; an advantage he was to keep to the flag.

1961 Ultra Lightweight T.T. (three laps - 113.19 miles)

Mike Hailwood   125 Honda   88.23 mph (record)

Leading riders had realised the tremendous potential provided by Honda, and Mike Hailwood, Luigi Taveri and Bob McIntyre joined the ranks. An entry of 58 had been received for the three-lap 125cc race, and of these 38 faced the starter at 10 a.m. on June 12th.

Honda riders had dominated practice, and it was no surprise when they filled five of the top six places at the end of the opening lap. Mike Hailwood set a new lap record from a standing start at 88.05 mph to lead Luigi Taveri by six seconds - Tom Phillis held third place with Jim Redman fourth. M.Z. rider Ernst Degner was fifth with Sadao Shimazaki on another Honda sixth. By the time lap two had been complet-

ed, Hondas filled all top six places, with Degner retiring at Handley's Corner.

Mike led Luigi by 11 seconds after setting a new lap record at 88.37 mph, Tom Phillis was still third, eight seconds down on the Swiss ace followed by Redman, Shimazaki and Taniguchi.

Taveri really flew on the last lap and raised the lap record to 88.45 mph, but 'Mike the Bike' won at a new record speed of 88.23 mph by 7.4 seconds with Phillis, Redman and Shimazaki completing the top five - Taniguchi took eighth place. The first three took the Manufacturers award for Honda. The dream of 1954 had become a reality.

The start of an era; The winners (left to right), Tom Phillis, Luigi Taveri and Mike Hailwood.

Unswerving concentration is etched on Mike Hailwood's face as he lines up for Quarter Bridge.

1961 Lightweight T.T. (five laps - 188.65 miles)

Mike Hailwood   249 Honda   98.38 mph (record)

At 3p.m. the same day, 47 riders lined up for the start of the five-lap Lightweight T.T. There was a sensational start when Bob McIntyre took his Honda round at almost 100 mph from a standing start - 98.38 mph - and led Gary Hocking (MV Agusta) by 25 seconds with Hailwood's Honda in third place followed by Tom Phillis, Jim Redman and Kunimitsu Takahashi.

On lap two McIntyre raised the lap record to 99.58 mph, and led Hailwood by 36 seconds, with Hocking dropping to third. Bob continued to lead at the end of lap three from Mike, but Tom Phillis took third place when Hocking retired, so Honda filled all top six places.

There were no changes to the leaderboard at the end of the fourth lap. But on the final circuit, Bob McIntyre retired at Sulby with engine trouble, so Mike Hailwood completed a double on the same day for Honda at a record 98.38 mph, followed by team mates Tom Phillis, Jim Redman, Kunimitsu Takahashi and Naomi Taniguchi.

Honda took the Manufacturers award for the performances of Redman, Takahashi and Taniguchi, and for good measure Hailwood, Redman and Phillis took the Club Team award for Southampton & D.M.C.C.

Fred Stevens at Signpost Corner on his fully road-equipped CB72. Fred was the first rider to start a T.T. race using an electric start; he finished thirteenth, ahead of many full racing machines.

Bob McIntyre gets the thumbs up to start practice on his Honda-4

With the flag in sight - Derek Minter squirts the Honda out of Governors

1962 Lightweight T.T. (six laps - 226.38 miles)

Derek Minter   249 Honda   96.68 mph

The Lightweight Race for 1962 was increased to six laps - 226.38 miles.

Bob McIntyre set the pace from the start with a lap at 99.06 mph and led Jim Redman by half a minute with Derek Minter, Tom Phillis and Moto Kitano - all on Hondas - taking third to fifth places, with the Benelli of Mike Hailwood in sixth place. Bob McIntyre went out on the second lap which saw Redman lead from Phillis with Hailwood up to third spot. At half distance Minter was in the lead by by 15 seconds, but a 52 second pit stop was a problem. Redman went straight through and by the time the fourth lap had been completed the Southern Rhodesian had a 31-second advantage. But Jim was having trouble with the fuel cap on his machine, it kept popping open, he was losing petrol and he had to stop at the end of the fifth lap to take on extra fuel.

Derek Minter took full advantage and went on to win his first T.T. race by almost two minutes. Jim Redman and Tom Phillis ensured a Honda 1-2-3, and there were just eight finishers and only four replicas were won - Arthur Wheeler (Guzzi) was fourth and Mike Hailwood retired on the last lap.

'King of Brands' becomes 'Prince of the T.T.'. Derek Minter receives the Mercury trophy from T. Albert Corkish, Mayor of Douglas.

Australian Tom Phillis accelerates out of Quarter Bridge. Third in this race, Tom was fatally injured in the Junior race, two days later.

Signpost style from Luigi Taveri

1962 Ultra Lightweight T.T. (three laps - 113.19 miles)

Luigi Taveri   125 Honda   89.88 mph   (record)

Thirty-eight starters lined up for the three lap 125cc race and Hondas were firm favourites to take the honours judging by practice form, with only the E.M.C. of Mike Hailwood expected to mount any sort of challenge.

Taveri took the lead from the flag and at the end of the first 37 miles, with a lap record at 89.79 mph, had an advantage of 21 seconds over Hailwood with the Hondas of Jim Redman, Tommy Robb, Tom Phillis and Derek Minter in hot pursuit.

Taveri went even faster on his second lap and raised the lap record to 90.13 mph, the first 90 mph plus lap in the Ultra-Lightweight and increased his lead to 44 seconds, Hailwood was still third but Robb had overtaken Phillis.

On to the final lap and Luigi Taveri made no mistake, he didn't break the lap record again, but won at a new record race speed of 89.88 mph, by 66 seconds from Tommy Robb with Tom Phillis in third place and Hondas completed the top five through Derek Minter and Jim Redman. Hailwood's brave challenge ended on the last lap at Glen Helen.

Belfast's Tommy Robb gained the first of his leaderboard places on this 125, seen on the Glencrutchery Road.

A large trophy for a small man! Luigi Taveri is almost dwarfed by the Ultra Lightweight T.T. trophy.

The first of six - Jim Redman - Quarter Bridge

1963 Lightweight T.T. (six laps - 226.38 miles)

Jim Redman   250 Honda   94.85 mph

This race saw the start of a remarkable run of success by Jim Redman. There were 53 starters for the six-lap race, and it was Yamaha riders Fumio Ito and Tony Godfrey who led at the end of the first lap from the Hondas of Jim Redman, Luigi Taveri, Kunimitsu Takahashi and Bill Smith.

Redman got his race face on on the second lap and closed to within one second of the leader Ito, Godfrey had stopped for adjustments and dropped to seventh.

T.T. history was made on lap three when Tony Godfrey crashed at Milntown and became the first rider to be picked up by the rescue helicopter. At the end of the lap Redman was in command by 18 seconds from Ito. Luigi Taveri had retired so Bill Smith brought his Honda into third place. New to the leaderboard were John Kidson (Guzzi) and Jack Findlay (DMW) and Tommy Robb brought his Honda into sixth place. Findlay had a spill at Greeba Bridge on the next lap and retired.

Jim Redman stayed in command to the chequered flag and won by 27.2 seconds from Fumio Ito with Bill Smith third. Hiroshi Hasegawa brought his Yamaha into fourth place ahead of Tommy Robb.

A T.T. veteran, Liverpool dealer Bill Smith enjoyed a long success on Honda machinery in the T.T.. On his production racer, he peels into Quarter Bridge.

Kunimitsu Takahashi accelerates out of Governors Bridge. 'Kuni-san' was the first Japanese rider to win a Grand Prix, the 1961 250 German GP.

Four down - two to go for Jim Redman, pictured on the first lap at Quarter Bridge

1963 Junior T.T. (six laps - 226.38 miles)

Jim Redman   350 Honda   94.91 mph

There was quite an international flavour amongst the 77 machines that lined up for the Junior T.T. Honda's Jim Redman and Tommy Robb were facing the MV Agusta of Mike Hailwood, the Gileras of John Hartle and Phil Read and the Jawa of Franta Stastny.

Redman led at the end of the opening lap by 0.8 of a second from Mike Hailwood with the Gileras of Hartle and Read chasing hard. Tommy Robb was in seventh place. The Irishman retired however on lap two and Redman set the fastest lap of the race at 101.30 mph to consolidate his lead. Phil Read also went out on the second lap so Sid Mizen (A.J.S.) and Jim Rae (Norton) came into the top six. At half distance the race order was Redman, Hailwood, Hartle and Stastny. Hailwood's race ended on lap four when he was reported to be touring.

So Jim Redman completed a 250/350cc double from John Hartle and Franta Stastny. Sid Mizen, Jack Ahearn (Norton) and Mike Duff (A.J.S.) completed the top six.

Tommy Robb at Quarter Bridge.

The Swiss star aviates at Ballaugh Bridge

1964 Ultra Lightweight T.T. (three laps - 113.19 miles)

Luigi Taveri **125 Honda** **92.14 mph** (record)

Honda completed their first hat-trick of wins this year when the Swiss ace took the three-lap 125cc race - and it was a cracking event.

At the end of the opening lap it was Jim Redman in the lead by 0.2 seconds from Frank Perris on the Suzuki with Taveri just three seconds down in third place and Ralph Bryans (Honda) was in fourth place.

Perris retired on the second lap and Redman's lead was now up to 12 seconds from Taveri while Bryans made it a Honda top three. Jim Redman was first to finish and it looked as if he had won three in a week - but Luigi had other ideas.

On the final lap he hurled the little Honda around the course and smashed the lap record - he lapped at 93.53 mph to snatch victory from his team mate by just three little seconds!! Ralph Bryans held on to third place, S. Malina (CZ) was fourth and Scheimann and Beale finished fifth and sixth on their Hondas. In fact from the 18 replica winners, 16 rode Hondas.

Bryans, Redman and Taveri gave Honda the Manufacturers Team award.

After yet another Honda 1-2-3, Redman, Taveri and Bryans discuss the race.

Second successive Lightweight win for the popular Southern Rhodesian

1964 Lightweight T.T. (six laps - 226.38 miles)

Jim Redman   250 Honda   97.45 mph

The main Honda riders in a field of 64, were Jim Redman and Luigi Taveri, with opposition likely to come from Phil Read, Tarquinio Provini and Alan Shepherd.

At the end of the opening lap it was Redman in front by three seconds from Read with Alan Shepherd on the M.Z. in third place. Taveri had his Honda tucked into fourth place and was followed by Tarquinio Provini (Benelli) and Jack Ahearn (Suzuki). Read slowed on lap two and was passed by Shepherd and Taveri, and Redman's lead was up to 10 seconds. Next time around Provini was also ahead of Read, but Taveri slowed and dropped to fifth and had a three minute pit stop during which the complete ignition system was changed. Read led at the end of lap four but only reached Quarter bridge before retiring, so Jim Redman took over again and at the end of lap five led Shep-

herd and Malina (M.Z.).

Taveri and Provini retired so Redman completed a Lightweight double by 41 seconds from Shepherd and they were the only two riders to win silver replicas!! Alberto Pagani brought his Paton into third place ahead of Malina - there were just eight finishers.

Luigi Taveri was king of the small machines, but he was capable of riding the bigger models with great elan. Here, he takes the 250-4 round Ramsey Hairpin.

Impeccable style from Jim Redman at Governors Bridge hairpin

1964 Junior T.T. (six laps - 226.38 miles)

Jim Redman   350 Honda   98.50 mph

Jim Redman's main challenger Mike Hailwood was a non-starter for the Junior due to illness, so Redman was the firm favourite for a "double double".

He led from start to finish without having to break any records. Alan Shepherd on the M.Z, was second after the first circuit by 14 seconds but he retired on lap two. This brought Franta Stastny (Jawa) up to second place but he was 53 seconds down on the Honda star. The lead was over one minute at half distance and then Stastny went out at the Bungalow, and Mike Duff (A.J.S.) took over second place, but over five minutes down with two laps to go. By the time they started their last lap Jim Redman led Mike Duff by over six minutes but Phil Read (A.J.S.) was only one second down on the second place man.

Redman completed his second Junior win by seven minutes and 14 seconds, but from Read who pipped Duff for the runner-up spot by 12 seconds. Bruce Beale won a silver replica for 11th place on his Honda.

Jim Redman prepares for a practice lap. For the race itself, he took Tommy Robb's number 6, having less traffic to pass on his way to victory.

Bruce Beale, a South African compatriot of Jim Redman, swings his production racer 305 model into Parliament Square.

Jim Redman at the 'other' hairpin - Ramsey

1965 Lightweight T.T. (six laps - 226.38 miles)

Jim Redman   250 Honda   97.19 mph

A Japanese battle was on the cards for the Lightweight T.T. with Honda, Yamaha and Suzuki all out to take the trophy East.

At the end of lap one Phil Read (Yamaha) set the first 100 mph plus lap on a 250 - 100.01 mph - to lead Jim Redman by 15 seconds with Yamaha's Bill Ivy in third place followed by Duff (Yamaha), Provini (Benelli) and Perris (Suzuki). Read's machine developed engine problems on lap two and he retired at the Mountain Box. Redman had got the message that he was second and set a new lap record on this lap at 100.09 mph and led Ivy by 36 seconds, Mike Duff was third and Franta Stastny brought his Jawa into sixth place.

Redman's lead after lap three had been completed was up to almost a minute. On lap four Bill Ivy came off at Brandywell and Perris took over third place whilst Bruce Beale brought his Honda into sixth place. With one lap to go Jim Redman led Mike Duff by over three minutes and sailed on to complete a hat-trick of Lightweight wins by three minutes 41 seconds from Duff with Perris in third place. Bruce Beale lost his top six place when he retired on the last lap.

Bruce Beale's luck ran out in the Lightweight race; he was to fare better in the Junior.

A group of Honda technicians run up Jim Redman's 250-6. Nobby Clark (right) has been working on these models in the '90s. The bikes are now owned by Rob Iannucci in America.

Heading for his sixth win - Jim Redman at Ginger Hall

1965 Junior T.T. (six laps - 226.38 miles)

Jim Redman   350 Honda   100.72 mph (record)

Jim Redman sat on the start line among 93 riders knowing he could make history by winning for the third year in succession to add to his three Lightweight wins. But what opposition he faced. Mike Hailwood and newcomer Giacomo Agostini on the M.V. Agusta and Phil Read on the Yamaha.

He knew it was going to be tough when the first lap times were posted - with a new lap record at 102.85 mph Hailwood led him by 20 seconds with Phil Read in third place followed by Agostini, Woodman (M.Z.) and Stastny (Jawa). The top three remained the same after two laps, and at half distance the Grandstand crowds were agog as Hailwood, leading by 28 seconds, and Redman came in to refuel together. Jim made a rapid stop and flew away, but Mike was in for three minutes before the M.V. fired up. He only got as far as Sarah's Cottage before retiring, so Jim took over his customary first place and at the end of lap four led Read by 76 seconds with Derek Woodman in third place.

The reliability of the Honda gave Jim Redman his sixth and final T.T. victory

by one minute 52 seconds from Phil Read - Derek Woodman went out on the last lap and Giacomo Agostini took third place on his T.T. debut. Another fine ride by Bruce Beale gave him fourth place on his Honda.

In the Castle Mona garage, Nobby Clark (left) discusses brakes with Michihiko Aika and Ralph Bryans (right). 'Aika-san' was the chief mechanic during the golden years of the works machines.

Taveri 'flat' on Bray Hill

1965 50cc T.T. (three laps - 113.19 miles)

Luigi Taveri   50 Honda   79.66 mph

Honda added to their list of trophies with their first win in the three-lap 50cc 'Tiddlers' Race.

The conditions were poor so any record breaking was out of the question. Mitsuo Itoh (Suzuki) led Taveri at the end of the first lap by 12 seconds followed by the Suzukis of Hugh Anderson and Ernst Degner, Ralph Bryans (Honda) and Charlie Mates (Honda). Ralph's race ended in retirement on the second lap, which saw Taveri take the lead, but from Anderson.

Itoh came into the pits, made adjustments and got away but only made it as far as Greeba before the machine cried enough.

Luigi made no mistake on the final lap and set the fastest lap of the race at 80.80 mph to win his third T.T. Race from Hugh Anderson by almost a minute with Ernst Degner in third place, whilst Mates brought his Honda home in fourth place.

Ralph Bryans hugs the wall at Union Mills. This race ended in a retirement, but he took revenge the next year.

The master at work - Hailwood at White Gates, Ramsey

1966 Lightweight T.T. (six laps - 226.38 miles)

Mike Hailwood   **250 Honda**   **101.79 mph** (record)

This was the year the T.T. faced a major crisis. A national seamans strike meant that it had to be postponed, but co-operation between all concerned saw the dates moved to late August/early September.

Mike Hailwood, with seven T.T. victories to his credit, was back with Honda for 1966, ably backed by Stuart Graham, son of the 1953 Ultra Lightweight winner Les. Mike made his mark from the off, smashing the lap record at 104.29 mph to lead Yamaha's Phil Read by 39 seconds with Graham in third place. Phil Read went out at Ginger Hall on lap two to leave Hailwood leading Bill Ivy (Yamaha) by one minute 49 seconds with Graham still third.

At half distance there were no problems for Hailwood, but that could not be said for his immediate pursuers - Graham had difficulty firing up after his refuelling and Ivy stopped for 90 seconds and changed a plug. The order for the next two laps was Hailwood, Graham and Ivy, but the Yamaha rider pulled in at the end of lap five to retire. Hailwood logged up win number eight by over five minutes from Graham and Peter Inchley brought his Villiers into third place ahead of Stastny's Jawa.

A well earned drink - Mick Woollett of Motorcycle News (left) and Leslie Nicholl, Daily Express (right) wait whilst Mike gets the vocal cords lubricated to give his first-hand account of the race.

Stuart Graham rounds Quarter Bridge on the Honda-6.

Man and machine in miniature - Ralph Bryans, the fastest ever 50cc rider on the Mountain Course, negotiates Governors Bridge

1966 50cc T.T. (three laps - 113.19 miles)

Ralph Bryans   **50 Honda**   **85.66 mph** (record)

This race attracted just 17 entries and it was a massed start event. The entry may have been small but the quality was there.

On the opening lap Luigi Taveri and Ralph Bryans on the Hondas were almost side by side for the first 30 miles, but then Bryans turned up the wick and led his team-mate by six seconds at the end of the lap, followed by the Suzukis of Katayama, Anscheidt, Anderson and Degner.

On his second lap Ralph Bryans set a record at 85.66 mph, a record that would never be beaten and added another 18 seconds to his advantage. Anscheidt retired on Bray Hill on lap two and Tommy Robb brought his Suzuki into sixth place. Ralph Bryans won his first T.T. at a record speed over Taveri by 51.2 seconds to give Honda their second successive win in the smallest class at the meeting, and Bryans, Taveri and Dave Simmonds won the Manufacturers award.

The Honda 50cc dream team - Bryans leads Taveri at Quarter Bridge on the first lap.

Mike sweeps the mighty Honda round Signpost Corner

1966 Senior T.T. (six laps - 226.38 miles)

Mike Hailwood   500 Honda   103.11 mph

A Japanese/Italian battle was forecast for the Senior T.T. - Honda v. M.V. Agusta, - Hailwood versus Agostini - these were the two riders among the 81 starters who the fans were concentrating on.

Hailwood opened with a lap at 105.82 mph to lead his Italian rival by six seconds, with Peter Williams (Matchless) in third place a further two minutes down, followed by Malcolm Uphill (Norton), John Blanchard (Matchless) and Jack Ahearn (Norton).

Agostini broke the lap record second time around, but Mike went even faster - 107.07 mph - and increased his lead to 13 seconds, Uphill was third after Williams dropped off the leaderboard. At half distance Hailwood led by 22 seconds, and Blanchard was the new third placed man after Uphill's retirement at the Highlander. Agostini trailed Hailwood by 56 seconds after four laps had been completed, and Chris Conn took third place from Blanchard.

So Mike notched up his ninth win on the T.T. Course and left an absolute lap record at 107.07 mph to be challenged in Diamond Jubilee Year, and only rain in the latter stages of the race prevented him from setting a new race record.

Mike Hailwood (Honda, 2) sits astride the mighty 500-4 and contemplates another battle with Giacomo Agostini (MV, 6) - a battle which Mike was to convincingly win.

The sweet sound of the Honda-6 reverberates through Ramsey

1967 Lightweight T.T. (six laps - 226.38 miles)

Mike Hailwood   250 Honda   103.07 mph (record)

Diamond Jubilee Year - celebrating 60 glorious years of T.T. Racing - and celebrations also for Stanley Michael Bailey Hailwood!! His first race of the week was the six lap Lightweight T.T. - and a chance to equal Stanley Woods record of 10 wins on the T.T. Course.

The opening lap was a real cracker with just 2.5 seconds covering the first three - and it was Mike in front followed by the Yamahas of Phil Read and Bill Ivy while Hailwood's team-mate Ralph Bryans was in the top six. Lap two saw a new lap record from Mike - 104.50 mph - and he led Read by 13 seconds with Ivy a further nine seconds down.

Lap three saw no changes but Bryans was closing in on the top three. Bill Ivy went out on lap four, Bryans took over third spot and Mike led the race by 38 seconds.

The top three maintained their positions to the finish and Mike won from Phil by a minute and a half. The first person to congratulate Mike on his 10th win was the great Stanley Woods, whose record he had equalled and the Irishman was genuinely delighted that Mike had reached this landmark in his first race at the Diamond Jubilee.

A historic moment; Mike Hailwood seems almost embarrassed as he receives the congratulations of 10-times T.T. winner Stanley Woods (right); Stan Hailwood, Mike's father stands on the left.

The blazing sunshine and melting tar makes Ralph Bryans take a near vertical style through Signpost Corner.

Another record-breaking win for Hailwood - Signpost Corner

1967 Junior T.T. (six laps - 226.38 miles)

Mike Hailwood   297 Honda   104.68 mph (record)

During practice for the Junior Mike had broken the lap record at 103.24 mph - so could anyone stop him notching up win number 11? The answer was an emphatic NO!

He opened proceedings with a lap at 107.73 mph, not only a Junior lap record - but an absolute lap record.

He left the M.V.'s, MZ's, Benelli's and Aermacchi's trailing in his wake. In second place at the end of the lap was Agostini on the M.V. - already 49 seconds down and Renzo Pasolini had his Benelli in third place. The top six was completed by Heinz Rosner (M.Z.), Fred Stevens (Paton) and Derek Woodman (M.Z.). On lap two Mike slowed slightly - he only lapped at 107.49 mph! - but his lead over Agostini was up to 63 seconds. No changes to the top six on the third lap and Mike led the race by by over two minutes. Two of the top six went out on lap four - Rosner at Ballaugh and Pasolini at Creg-ny-Baa.

Mike went on to notch up win number eleven by over three minutes from Agostini as Woodman took third place.

'Mike the Bike'

Mike leaves Governors Bridge

The mighty Honda - the mighty Mike - in unison at Governors Bridge

1967 Senior T.T. (six laps - 226.38 miles)

Mike Hailwood   500 Honda   105.62 mph (record)

Mike faced a strong challenge in his attempt to score his second hat-trick of wins in the final race of Diamond Jubilee week. Agostini on the M.V. had lapped in practice at 106.56 mph, and he set the crowd alight with an opening lap at 108.30 mph, a new absolute lap record, and led Mike by 12 seconds. These two superstars had already left the rest of the field miles behind. Mike got the message and on lap two raised the record to an amazing 108.77 mph and reduced the Italian's lead to eight seconds.

They flashed around the Mountain Circuit on lap three and when they came in for fuel, Mike had clawed back another six seconds - just two seconds between them at half distance. But Mike had a problem with a loose twist grip, he called for a hammer, and literally bashed it tight himself. This gave Agostini the spurt he needed and at the end of lap four he led the race by 12 seconds. But the race ended for him, on his birthday too, when the chain snapped at Windy Corner and he freewheeled into the Grandstand.

Mike had the race in the bag now and won by almost eight minutes from Peter Williams (Arter Matchless) and Steve Spencer (Lancefield Norton). Mike retired from motorcycle racing at the end of the year but he left a target of 12 wins and an absolute lap record which would stand for quite a while.

Mike gives the 500-4 a big heave to start six record-breaking laps

Bill Penny gave Honda their first Production Race win

1969 Production 500 (three laps - 113.19 miles)

Bill Penny   444 Honda   88.18 mph

There were 14 starters for the 500cc Class of the three-lap Production Race and it was the Kawasaki of Tony Dunnell who led at the end of the first lap by 37 seconds from Bill Penny (Honda CB450) who in turn had an advantage of five seconds over Ray Knight (Triumph).

Eddie Johnson (Suzuki), Ron Baylie (Triumph) and Adrian Cooper (Suzuki) completed the top six. Two of the top six, leader Dunnell and Johnson retired on lap two, and Penny took command of the race by 21 seconds from Knight who was over one minute up on Baylie.

Bill Penny made no mistake and went on to win by 28.6 seconds from Knight while Baylie held on to his third place. Cooper finished fourth ahead of Hugh Evans (B.S.A.) and Mick Chatterton (Triumph) and these top six finishers were the only ones to receive silver replicas.

Bill Penny, out in front at Braddan Bridge

Bill Smith led from start to finish

1971 Production 250 (four laps - 150.92 miles)

Bill Smith **249 Honda** **84.14 mph**

Fourteen riders lined up for the start of this four-lap race and Bill Smith led throughout on his Honda CB250. After the opening lap he led Charlie Williams (Yamaha) by 13 seconds with Tommy Robb on another Honda CB250 in third place some 2.4 seconds down on Williams.

Despite the challenge of a posse of Suzuki riders, amazingly the top three remained the same for the four laps. Lap two saw Williams knock a second of Smith's lead and Robb was five seconds down. Bill Smith opened the taps third time around and led Charlie by 27 seconds and Tommy was now 45 seconds down in third place.

On the final circuit Williams set the fastest lap of the race - 84.64 mph but it was to no avail, Bill Smith took the trophy by nine seconds with Tommy Robb in third place almost two minutes down.

Bill Barker leaves Governors Bridge on his way to 9th place.

No time to read the inscription on the Guthrie Memorial - John Williams speeds to a record win

1971 Production 500 (four laps - 150.92 miles)

John Williams   450 Honda   91.04 mph (record)

There were 17 starters for the four-lap race and John Williams on the Honda CB450 shot into the lead from the flag and was never passed throughout the race.

After lap one he was 2.2. seconds ahead of Roger Bowler (Triumph) who in turn was 11 seconds up on Gordon Pantall (Suzuki). They were followed by Bill Penny (Honda), Graham Bailey (Suzuki) and Adrian Cooper (Suzuki). The top three maintained station on lap two and the time differences were up to seven and 23 seconds.

Williams really stamped his authority on the race over the last two laps - he led Bowler by 38 seconds after lap three and Pantall trailed in third place by 30 seconds.

John Williams set a new lap record on the final circuit at 91.45 mph to win from Bill Penny by two minutes 11 seconds and Adrian Cooper finished third. Both Bowler and Pantall retired on this last lap so the Suzukis of Graham Bailey, Tom Loughridge and Martin Ashwood completed the top six.

Second place this time for Bill Penny

John Williams shows winning style at Creg ny Baa

Another 'proddy' win for "J. W."

1972 Production 250 (four laps - 150.92 miles)

John Williams   **250 Honda**   **85.32 mph** (record)

John Williams took the honours comfortably on his Honda CB250 - he led all the way with the main challenge coming from Charlie Williams on his Yamaha who was second throughout the four laps.

After lap one John was 12 seconds ahead of Charlie with Eddie Roberts (Suzuki) a further 40 seconds down. Danny Shimmin (Suzuki), Mal Kirwan (Bultaco) and Dave Arnold (Ducati) completed the top six.

With the fastest lap of the race, John's lead at half distance was up to 33 seconds and Roberts was still third, but now 54 seconds down on Charlie. Over one minute was John's advantage over Charlie after lap three, and Danny Shimmin had taken third place from Eddie Roberts.

So to the final lap and John took his Honda to victory by a margin of 90 seconds over Charlie. Danny Shimmin retired on the last lap so Eddie Roberts regained his third place. Dave Arnold finished fourth, Neil Tuxworth, now Honda Team manager, was fifth with John Evans taking the final leaderboard place.

Keith Heckles hurries the CB 250 out of Governors.

Long-time Honda enthusiast John Kiddie at Braddan Bridge.

Concentration from the victor - Bill Smith

1973 Production 500 (four laps - 150.92 miles)

Bill Smith   500 Honda   88.10 mph

At the end of the first of the four laps it was Stan Woods (Suzuki) who led Bill Smith (Honda) by four seconds who in turn had a 41-second advantage over Danny Shimmin (Suzuki), he was followed on the leaderboard by Keith Martin (Kawasaki), Alex George (Kawasaki) and Bill Milne (Kawasaki).

Smith lapped nine seconds faster than Woods on lap two to take over the lead by five seconds with Shimmin, Martin and Clive Brown (B.S.A.) next on the leaderboard. Stan Woods set a new lap record on lap three - 94.44 mph - and closed to just one second of Bill Smith with Shimmin, Brown and Martin still disputing the lower leaderboard places.

But Bill Smith got the message and upped the power on the final 37.73 miles to take the flag 8.2 seconds ahead of Stan Woods, Danny Shimmin went out on the final lap so Keith Martin took third place, Clive Brown finished fourth ahead of Roger Bowler (Triumph) and Bill Milne.

For many years the holder of the greatest number of T.T. replicas, Bill Smith adds to his collection as he leaves Governors Bridge and heads for the chequered flag.

A winning T.T. return for Phil Read

1977 Formula 1 (four laps - 150.92 miles)

Phil Read   820 Honda   97.02 mph

T.T. Formula World Championships were introduced to the programme in 1977 and Honda won all three.

In the five-lap Formula 1 race there was a surprise return to the T.T. Races by Phil Read, his first appearance since 1972. He had lost none of his flair, and led Stan Woods (Honda) at the end of the opening lap by 28 seconds with the Ducati of Roger Nicholls 46 seconds down in third place. Tom Herron (Ducati), Mick Poxon (Trident) and Ian Richards (Honda) completed the top six. Lap two saw Read, with the fastest lap of the race at 101.74 mph, increase his lead over Nicholls who had overtaken Woods.

The weather began to worsen by the time lap three had been completed and Roger Nicholls put in a real flyer to snatch the lead from Read by just two seconds. Nicholls stopped to refuel but Read went straight through, so was now leading the race.

But then it was announced that because of the very wet conditions the race would be stopped at the end of the fourth lap - so Phil Read became the first ever T.T. Formula 1 World Champion by 38.4 seconds, Ian Richards took third spot ahead of Stan Woods, Malcolm Lucas (B.S.A.) and Michael Hunt (Laverda).

Just look at the weather! Ian Richards splashes out of the Governors Bridge dip onto Glencrutchery Road at the end of the fourth and last lap.

A lap at over the ton helped Alan Jackson to victory

1977 Formula 2 (four laps - 150.92 miles)

Alan Jackson   598 Honda   99.36 mph

There were just 14 starters for the four-lap Formula 2 Race, run concurrently with the Formula 3 event. Frank Rutter (Honda) set the early pace and led Bill Smith (Honda) by six seconds at the end of lap one, with Ian Richards (Honda) in third place, and Alan Jackson completed a Honda top four.

On lap two Frank Rutter and Ian Richards both retired and Alan Jackson, with the fastest lap of the race at 101.15 mph, jumped from fourth to first and led Bill Smith by four seconds and Neil Tuxworth (Honda) took third place. Another new leader at the end of the third lap - Bill Smith - with an advantage of over half a minute over Alan Jackson.

But Bill was not destined to add to his list of victories, he retired on the final lap at Ballaugh, so Alan Jackson took the first ever F2 World Championship by one minute 24 seconds from Neil Tuxworth who finished two minutes 26 seconds ahead of the third place man Dennis Casement (Honda), and only these top three received silver replicas.

Neil Tuxworth - a fine second place.

John Kidson takes the first F3 title

1977 Formula 3 (four laps - 150.92 miles)

John Kidson   **398 Honda**   **93.28 mph**

Twenty-one riders lined up for this race, which started after the Formula 2.

Hondas in the hands of John Kidson and John Stephens set the pace, Kidson had an advantage of 10 seconds over Stephens at the end of the first lap with the Suzuki of Brian Peters in third place. The order remained the same on lap two, but Kidson had added another nine seconds to his lead. John

Stephens set the fastest third lap - 30 seconds faster than Kidson - and took the lead by 11 seconds.

But on the final lap his race ended in a retirement at Kirk Michael so the first F3 crown went to John Kidson by over five minutes from Brian Peters with Alan Walsh (Honda) just nine seconds down in third place. Graham Bentman (Honda), Fred Launchbury (Maico) and Mal Kirwan (Honda) collected bronze replicas for fourth to sixth places.

Third place man Alan Walsh sets up his bike for the fast right-hander at Ballacraine.

Two in a row for Alan Jackson

1978 Formula 2 (four laps - 150.92 miles)

Alan Jackson   598 Honda   99.35 mph

Alan Jackson completed a double when he won the four-lap Formula 2 race - and for consistency he took just 0.6 seconds longer than he had the previous year!! yet set a new lap record.

At the end of the opening lap he was 18 seconds ahead of Dave Mason (Honda) with Frank Rutter (Honda) 12 seconds down in third spot. Neil Tuxworth (Honda), Ron Haslam (Honda) and Joey Dunlop (Benelli) completed the first lap leaderboard. Lap two saw Jackson increase his lead over Mason to 37 seconds, Frank Rutter had a 45-minute lap, dropped down the charts and retired. This brought Tuxworth up to third place, 44 seconds down on Mason, with Haslam and Dunlop climbing one place each.

Pit stops altered the order of the race, and lap three saw Mason 21 seconds ahead of Jackson with Tuxworth still third.

On the last lap Alan Jackson broke the lap record at 103.21 mph to win from Dave Mason by one minute 34 seconds, the next four on the leaderboard remained the same and Peter Davies (Laverda) took sixth place.

Ron Haslam started his T.T. career in the Formula races; Manx Radio's commentator Geoff Cannell was critical of his style at Ballaugh Bridge.

Dave Mason at Sulby Bridge.

Honda - The T.T. Winning Years 63

A record race win for Bill Smith

1978 Formula 3 (four laps - 150.92 miles)

Bill Smith   **398 Honda**   **94.47 mph**   (record)

Bill Smith made up for the disappointment of the previous year by taking the Formula 3 race win, again run concurrently with the Formula 2, winning from start to finish.

He led Dick Linton (Harley Davidson) by seven seconds after the first 37 miles, but Linton was just 0.2 seconds up on Peter Grove (Honda), four seconds further down was Derek Mortimer (Yamaha) who was just two seconds ahead of John Stephens (Honda). Dick Linton slowed on the second lap and then retired, Smith therefore led Grove with Mortimer third

and Stephens fourth.

By the time the third lap had been timed, Bill Smith was three minutes up on Derek Mortimer, Peter Grove had struck trouble and lapped in 48 minutes and retired.

So to the final lap - Bill Smith set a new lap record at 96.13 mph, and won from Mortimer by four minutes 41 seconds with John Stephens in third place.

The top six was completed by Mick Poxon (Honda), Alan Cathcart (Harley Davidson) and Fred Launchbury (Maico).

Third place for John Stephens, pictured at Braddan Bridge.

He flies through the air with the greatest of ease!! Alex George, Ballaugh Bridge

1979 Formula 1 (six laps - 226.38 miles)

Alex George　　　　**996 Honda**　　　　**110.57 mph** (record)

In 1979 the Island celebrated 1,000 years of it's Parliament - Tynwald - and the racing matched the occasion. The six lap T.T. Formula 1 race saw Alex George take over the mighty Honda, due to have been ridden by Mick Grant, but a pre-T.T. injury precluded the Yorkshireman from this race.

George grabbed his opportunity with both hands and with a lap record from a standing start at 111.95 mph, led at the end of the first lap by 24 seconds from Charlie Williams (Honda) and Ron Haslam had his Honda tucked in in third place. They were followed by Mike Hailwood (Ducati), who had made a dramatic return to the T.T. in 1978, Ian Richards (Honda) and

Graeme Crosby (Kawasaki). Alex went even faster on lap two - 112.94 mph - and increased his lead to 44 seconds.

These two maintained their positions to the chequered flag with Alex winning by almost one minute. But the battle for other leaderboard places was interesting. On lap three Hailwood took third place from Haslam - he held it on lap four - but after lap five Haslam snatched it back by just 1.4 seconds.

So Honda recorded another 1-2-3. Hailwood had problems on the last lap and finished fifth behind Graeme Crosby while Roger Bowler brought his Honda into sixth place.

Charlie Williams, who currently co-hosts Radio T.T., rode this David Dixon-prepared Yoshimura Honda to second place; here he passes through Parliament Square, Ramsey.

A hat-trick of F2 wins for Alan Jackson

1979 Formula 2 (four laps - 150.92 miles)

Alan Jackson   598 Honda   101.55 mph (record)

Alan Jackson was all out to give himself and Honda a hat-trick of wins in the four-lap T.T. Formula 2 race, but it was Frank Rutter (Honda) who led him at the end of the opening lap by 10 seconds and Dave Mason on another Honda was a further 10 seconds down in third place with Roger Bowler (Honda) fourth and Steve Tonkin (Honda) fifth.

Alan Jackson's response was swift - on lap two he set a new lap record at 104.40 mph to lead Rutter by five seconds - Mason retired second time around so Bowler took over third place just ahead of Tonkin.

The two leaders recorded almost identical times on lap three - Jackson was just 0.4 seconds faster than Rutter. On the final lap Frank Rutter retired. So Alan Jackson won from Roger Bowler by one minute and 42 seconds with Steve Tonkin in third place and Ian Richards fourth - the top four rode Hondas.

Steve Tonkin, heading for third place, at Quarter Bridge.

Mick Grant keeps a close eye on winner Alex George at Quarter Bridge

1979 Classic 1000cc (six laps - 226.38 miles)

Alex George   996 Honda   113.08 mph (record)

If ever a race lived up to it's title it was this one - a gigantic battle between the Honda of Alex George and the Suzuki of Mike Hailwood - there were other top riders in the field of 83 - but the eyes of the fans packed around the course focussed on the big two.

Lap one saw Alex nine seconds ahead of Mike - with the Yamahas of Bill Simpson, Charlie Williams and Joey Dunlop and the Suzuki of Steve Ward already losing touch. A brave effort by the injured Mick Grant on his Honda saw him holding seventh place. Hailwood lapped five seconds faster than Alex on lap two and the difference was down to four seconds.

Amazingly the two leaders recorded identical speeds on lap three - 114.14 mph - so the gap was still four seconds. Mick Grant's brave effort ended at the pits at half distance.

Lap four saw the end of Bill Simpson's race, and Alex was 3.4 seconds up on Hailwood with Charlie Williams still holding his third place. Lap five and at Ballacraine Mike led by half a second - at Ballaugh it was 1.4 seconds and at the Bungalow they were level! - and at the start of the last lap Mike led by 0.8 seconds. By Ballaugh Hailwood led by two seconds but by Ramsey it was down to 0.4 seconds. By the time the Mountain had been climbed for the final time George had grabbed the lead by 2.3 seconds. Mike crossed the line first, but Alex hung on to win by 3.4 seconds with a new lap record at 114.18 mph. That was to be Mike Hailwood's last ride in the T.T.

Charlie Williams finished third followed by the Yamahas of Jeff Sayle, Graeme McGregor and Joey Dunlop.

Mick Grant wheelies past a cottage at Rhencullen, a most spectacular yet accessible viewing spot for the T.T.. His injuries forced him out of the race.

The massed ranks of spectators watch Alex George beat off the challenge of Mike Hailwood to land the Formula 1 / Classic double.

Despite the conditions, Mick Grant took the trophy

1980 Formula 1 (six laps - 226.38 miles)

Mick Grant   999 Honda   105.29 mph

It would be fair to say that controversy surrounded this particular race - Alex George who had been No. 11 had a heavy crash on the final practice session and was out of the race. Suzuki applied for Graeme Crosby to take over his number, which would mean he started with Honda's Mick Grant. Honda protested but the start list remained - and the fans were happy with the thought of the two favourites blasting off together.

But it was the Honda of Graeme McGregor which led after lap one - by 12 seconds from Ron Haslam (Honda) with Crosby seven seconds down and just 0.6 seconds in front of Grant. Lap two saw dramatic changes - McGregor stopped at Kirk Michael for adjustments and retired at the end of the lap and

Haslam slipped down the leaderboard with exhaust problems and eventually retired at the end of lap three.

This left the big two to fight it out - at the end of lap two Grant was in front by 1.4 seconds - Crosby snatched the lead at the end of lap three but Grant snatched it back at the end of the fourth lap and held it to the chequered flag to win by 11 seconds from Crosby. Sammy McClements (Honda) finished third and set the fastest lap of the race on lap six at 106.88 mph. Alan Jackson and Mick Hunt (Kawasaki) and Keith Buckley (Honda) completed the top six.

But that wasn't the end of it - Suzuki lodged a protest about the size of Grant's tank - it was dismissed and the result stood.

Puddle-jumping - Honda style! Early race leader Graeme McGregor cautiously rounds Braddan Bridge.

Bill Smith at Douglas Corner, Kirk Michael.

A winner at last. Ron Haslam takes Governors Bridge

1982 Formula 1 (six laps - 226.38 miles)

Ron Haslam   999 Honda   113.33 mph (record)

Following the 1981 race, when Ron Haslam had been garlanded the winner, only to be relegated to second place when a protest from Suzuki claimed Graeme Crosby should be allowed the correct start time for having to start from the back of the field. The protest was upheld and Crosby was declared the winner with Haslam second, Honda star Haslam was all out to make amends in 1982.

This year also saw Joey Dunlop's first works ride for Honda. So to the race itself. Mick Grant had joined Suzuki and at the end of the opening lap, with a new lap record at 114.93 mph, he led by 19 seconds from Joey Dunlop with Ron Haslam one second down in third place. Dave Hiscock (Suzuki), Geoff Johnson (Kawasaki) and Roger Marshall (Suzuki) completed the top six. Mick increased his lead at the end of the second lap to 26 seconds, but it was now from Haslam who had taken the runner-up spot from Dunlop by 30 seconds.

This lap saw the end of Roger Marshall's race with a retirement, and Bernard Murray (Kawasaki) joined the top six. The top six remained static until the fifth lap when Mick Grant retired at Ramsey.

So Ron Haslam REALLY won his first T.T. Race by over four and a half minutes from Joey Dunlop with Dave Hiscock third - and a popular victory it was.

Honda riders Joey Dunlop, Ron Haslam and James Elbon took the Manufacturers award. The race will also be remembered for an amazing escape by George Fogarty, father of World Superbike star Carl. He crashed on Quarter Bridge Road after the very fast descent of Bray Hill, the bike burst into flames, he was unhurt and actually rode in the Senior race!

This picture is self-captioned! Joey at Quarter Bridge.

It's all smiles in the winners enclosure for Ron Haslam and a youthful looking Joey Dunlop.

First of six in a row for Joey

1983 Formula 1 (six laps - 226.38 miles)

Joey Dunlop   **850 Honda**   **114.03 mph** (record)

Joey Dunlop began a spectacular sequence of victories in the Formula 1 race when he won this year at a new race record.

At the end of the opening lap, with a new record at 115.73 mph, he led Mick Grant (Suzuki) by 18 seconds, who was followed by Geoff Johnson (Kawasaki) a further six seconds down, Rob McElnea (Suzuki), Roger Marshall (Honda) and Trevor Nation (Suzuki).

Surprisingly the order remained unchanged for the next two laps, and Joey still led comfortably despite a rear wheel change at his pit stop. On lap four McElnea took over third place from Johnson and Joey kept adding to his lead at the front, despite every effort from Mick Grant. The only lap that took Joey over 20 minutes in the race was lap five, which included his second pit stop, and the top six maintained station.

Joey won his first Formula 1 race by 53 seconds from Mick Grant who in turn was 13 seconds ahead of the third place man Rob McElnea. Geoff Johnson's luck ran out on the last lap when he retired, so Marshall took fourth place ahead of Nation and Sam McClements (Suzuki).

Honda took the Manufacturers Team prize through Dunlop, Marshall and Hartley Kerner who took 19th spot.

Hartley Kerner rounds Creg ny Baa on his VFR750; one of the Manufacturers prize winners with Joey and Roger Marshall.

Roger Marshall at Governors Bridge.

Fans admire the style of Joey at Governors

1984 Formula 1 (six laps - 226.38 miles)

Joey Dunlop   748 Honda   111.68 mph

Despite a very strong challenge from his Honda team-mate Roger Marshall, Joey Dunlop took his second successive Formula 1 title, and despite not breaking the race record, he did set a new lap record.

When the first lap times were posted they showed Joey 24 seconds up on Marshall with the Suzuki of Rob McElnea in third place just 1.4 seconds down. They were followed by Andy McGladdery (Kawasaki), Tony Rutter (Ducati) and Trevor Nation (Ducati). Lap two and Joey's lead was now up to 49 seconds with the top six the same. Rob McElnea had a slow third lap and dropped to eighth place, Marshall closed to within five seconds of Dunlop, and Jim Wells brought his Kawasaki into sixth place. No changes on lap four, but on lap five Roger Marshall took the lead from Joey - by just two little seconds.

Joey got the message alright and on his final lap he flew round at a new lap record speed of 115.89 mph to win by 8.9 seconds from Marshall, Tony Rutter held his steady third place. McGladdery finished fourth, Nation fifth and with the retirement of Jim Wells, Asa Moyce took his Kawasaki into sixth place.

Of the 26 finishers, 10 riders were on Hondas.

Roger Marshall ran Joey a close second.

The inquest starts. A post-race discussion between Joey and a Honda mechanic.

The final check on Trevor Nation's Honda

1984 Production 750 (three laps - 113.19 miles)

Trevor Nation   750 Honda   102.24 mph (record)

Hondas completely dominated this three-lap race, the first eight riders to finish rode the 750cc models and the battle at the front had the crowds on their toes for the entire 113.19 miles.

At the end of lap one it was the German star Helmut Dahne who led Trevor Nation, but by just 0.4 seconds - and 19 seconds down there was a tie for third place between Dave Dean and Hartley Kerner, they were two seconds ahead of Mark Salle who led Ken Dobson by 14 seconds. On lap two Nation set a new lap record at 102.97 mph to snatch the lead from Dahne by 1.2 seconds and Salle jumped up to third place ahead of Kerner and Dobson with Dean sixth.

On the final lap Trevor Nation lapped exactly one second faster than Helmut Dahne, to win by 2.2 seconds - Dave Dean put in a good last lap to take third place ahead of Hartley Kerner, Ken Dobson and Mark Salle. There were 27 finishers and 14 of them rode Hondas.

Trevor Nation at Braddan Bridge.

Joey, on for a hat-trick in the Formula One, caught in full flow at the Bungalow

1985 Formula 1 (six laps - 226.48 miles)

Joey Dunlop   748 Honda   113.95 mph

Joey was determined to make it a hat-trick of wins in the Formula 1 race, and he threw down the gauntlet on the opening lap by knocking 5.4 seconds of his own lap record - a speed of 116.43 mph.

This gave him a lead of some 29 seconds over his teammate Roger Marshall who held a slender 1.8 second advantage over the Suzuki of Mick Grant. Andy McGladdery (Suzuki), Steve Parrish (Yamaha) and Geoff Johnson (Yamaha) completed the first lap leaderboard. Joey added a further seven seconds to his lead after two laps had been completed, and the only change to the leaderboard was that Johnson retired.

Joey's lead at half distance was 40 seconds, and Tony Rutter, 10th on lap one moved up to sixth place. Lap four saw the end of Roger Marshall's race with a retirement at the Mountain Box, this allowed Mick Grant to take second place but well down on the leader. There were changes on lap five, Mick Grant went out with gearbox problems at Ballaugh, and Andy McGladdery had a spill at Cruickshanks Corner.

So the final leaderboard had a different look to it - Joey won from Tony Rutter by five minutes and 42 seconds. Steve Parrish finished third, but was excluded from the results because of an oversize tank, which promoted Sam McClements into the top three. In fourth place, after starting at No. 115 on his 749 Honda, was West German Superbike champion Peter Rubatto, a sensational ride by any standards. Dave Dean and Mark Salle on Suzukis completed the top six leaderboard.

A group of sun-drenched spectators get a birds' eye view as Peter Rubatto takes Signpost Corner, an impressive T.T. debut.

For years a member of the Honda team; Roger Marshall at Quarter Bridge.

Win number two of the 1985 races for the man from Ballymoney

1985 Junior T.T. (six laps - 226.38 miles)

Joey Dunlop   **247 Honda**   **109.90 mph** (record)

Joey Dunlop gave Honda their first 250cc T.T. victory since 1967 when he took the honours in the Junior Race, but he had to work hard for it.

At the end of the opening lap he was in the lead by 18 seconds from Brian Reid (Yamaha) with Steve Cull (Honda) in third place, three seconds down on the Yamaha rider. The leaderboard was completed by Gary Padgett (Honda), Gerry Brennan (E.M.C.) and Graham Cannell (Yamaha). Joey increased his lead at the end of the second lap by 2.8 seconds but refuelled whilst Reid went straight through and Cull was still third. Because of his pit stop Joey dropped down the lap three leaderboard which saw Reid in the lead by nine seconds from Cull with Joey third followed by Padgett, Cannell and Gene McDonnell (E.M.C.). Joey was back in front at the end of lap four with Reid chasing hard.

Hard indeed because on the fifth lap Reid shattered the lap record at 112.08 mph to lead Dunlop by 15 seconds. Eddie Roberts on the Kimoco was also tramping on and was in the top six, and Brennan retired on this lap. So a final lap with the two Irishmen all out for victory,

and another, Cull, keeping a close eye on proceedings.

But then drama struck - Brian Reid retired at Hillberry on the last lap - out of fuel. Joey won his second race of the week by 14.6 seconds from Steve Cull - another Honda 1-2, with Eddie Roberts in third place. Cannell, McDonnell and Johnny Rea (E.M.C.) completed the top six. Dunlop, Cull and Mick McGarrity gave Honda the Manufacturers award.

Steve Hislop, in his first year of T.T. racing, captured at Quarter Bridge on Ray Cowles' lightweight model.

Motor Cycle News road tester Mat Oxley took his only T.T. win in the Production 250

1985 Production 250 (three laps - 113.19 miles)

Mat Oxley   250 Honda   94.84 mph

Gary Padgett on the Padgett Honda set the early pace in this three-lap race, he led at the end of the first lap by 3.4 seconds from Mick McGarrity with Mat Oxley in third place 8.4 seconds down, then came Robert Dunlop, the first four were on Hondas, followed by Graham Cannell (Yamaha) and Phil Nicholls (Honda).

The top six remained the same on lap two, and Padgett had increased his lead over McGarrity to 3.6 seconds and Oxley, with the fastest second lap of the race, closed to within just one second of McGarrity.

The finishing flag was waiting for Gary Padgett, but he slid off at Governors Bridge - Mat Oxley had been burning up the circuit on the final lap and set a new record at 96.40 mph to snatch victory from Graham Cannell by 10.4 seconds - Pad-

gett picked himself up quickly and continued to take third place. McGarrity took fourth place followed by Phil Nicholls and a slowing Robert Dunlop completed the final top six leaderboard. Seven of the top eight were on Hondas.

An early Honda appearance for Robert Dunlop

So nearly a winner, Gary Padgett takes Quarter Bridge.

Highest yet? Geoff Johnson at Ballaugh Bridge

1985 Production 1500 (three laps - 113.19 miles)

Geoff Johnson   998 Honda   105.12 mph

Bill Simpson on the 900 Kawasaki led this race at the end of the opening lap from Geoff Johnson by 7.8 seconds and Kawasaki mounted Howard Selby was in third place a further 2.2 seconds down. Dennis Ireland and Dave Leach on Kawasakis were fourth and fifth with the 1000 Honda of Peter Linden in sixth place.

Simpson still led after two laps had been completed, but from Selby and by 13.4 seconds with Johnson in third place one second down - Ireland was still fourth but Linden over-took Leach for fifth place.

It was all down to the final 37.73 miles - Geoff Johnson had the bit between his teeth - he set the fastest of the third laps at 105.48 mph - he had started at No. 1 so finished first and had to wait for Simpson and Selby to complete the distance.

When the times were posted Johnson had won the race by just 3.2 seconds - from Simpson with Selby in third place - Ireland, Linden and Leach completed the top six.

Speedy Swede; Peter Linden takes the Gooseneck in fine style on his CB1000R.

Joey completes his first T.T. week hat-trick of wins with the Senior title

1985 Senior T.T. (six laps - 226.38 miles)

Joey Dunlop   750 Honda   113.69 mph

Could Joey Dunlop emulate the feat of Mike Hailwood and win three races in a week - it took just a couple of seconds under two hours to answer that question.

The opening lap saw him go straight into the lead from Klaus Klein (Suzuki) by 15.2 seconds with his Honda team-mate Roger Marshall in third place just 6.4 seconds down. Then came the Suzukis of Mark Johns, Mick Grant and Trevor Nation. Marshall overtook Klein on lap two and trailed Dunlop by 30 seconds - Klein was now third, Johns fourth, Nation fifth and Sammy McClements took sixth spot on his Suzuki - Mick Grant having retired after a spill at the Black Dub.

Half distance completed and Joey was 33.4 seconds up on Roger, McClements shot up to third ahead of Klein, Johns and Nation. The two Honda riders were separated by 32 seconds after the fourth lap times were posted, Johns was up to third ahead of McClements, and with the retirements of Trevor Nation and Klaus Klein on this lap, the latter after a spill at Glentramman, Barry Woodland and Andy McGladdery came into the top six. The top five stayed the same after five laps, and Steve Cull took sixth place from McGladdery. Roger Marshall set the fastest lap of the race on the final lap at 116.07 mph, but couldn't prevent Joey from completing his hat-trick - he won by 16.4 seconds with Mark Johns in third place and the rest of the top six remained unchanged.

Honda won the Manufacturers award through Dunlop, Marshall and eighth placed Roger Burnett.

Rothmans Honda team-mates Roger Marshall (left), at Governors Bridge and Roger Burnett (right) at Braddan Bridge.

An unusual inside shot of Joey at Ramsey Hairpin

1986 Formula 1 (four laps - 150.92 miles)

Joey Dunlop   750 Honda   112.96 mph

Joey eventually notched up his fourth successive Formula 1 win, but he had to wait until the Monday as the race was postponed from the Saturday because of bad weather.

Even on the Monday the weather wasn't all that good and the race distance was reduced to four laps. On the Rothmans Honda RVR/R, Joey led at the end of the first lap by 15.6 seconds from Geoff Johnson (Honda) with the Suzuki of Andy McGladdery in third place three seconds down.

Joey's team-mate Roger Marshall was fourth followed by Phil Mellor (Suzuki) and John Weeden (Suzuki). After lap two, Joey's lead over Johnson was up to 20 seconds, and Marshall took third place from McGladdery, Weeden and Mellor also swapped places.

Roger Marshall's race ended in retirement at Braddan Bridge on lap three, so Joey led Johnson by 42 seconds with McGladdery back up to third place, Weeden was fourth, Mellor fifth and Trevor Nation brought his Suzuki onto the leaderboard in sixth place.

On the fourth and final circuit Joey set the fastest lap of the race at 113.98 mph to win from Geoff by almost a minute and the rest of the top six remained the same.

Roger Marshall, who was out of luck in the Formula One race, hugs the kerb at Parliament Square

Saving front tyre wear!! Steve Cull gives spectators a spectacular close-up view at Rhencullen

1986 Junior T.T. (six laps - 226.38 miles)

Steve Cull   249 Honda   109.62 mph

Gary Padgett (Padgett Special) set the early pace in the six-lap Junior. He led Brian Reid (Kimoco) at the end of the opening lap by 1.6 seconds with Steve Cull in third place 2.8 seconds down. Phil Mellor (E.M.C.), Dave Leach (Yamaha) and Gene McDonnell (E.M.C.) completed the top six. Joey Dunlop most unusually slid off at Sulby Bridge on the opening lap due to a leaking fuel cap, he remounted but retired at the pits.

Lap two saw Padgett increase his lead to 10.2 seconds, but from Cull - Brian Reid had come off at Ballaugh Bridge. Leach was third, Mellor fourth, McDonnell fifth and Graham Cannell (Honda) took sixth spot.

At half distance Padgett's lead was 9.6 seconds from Cull with Mellor third. Leach was fourth, John Weeden (Armstrong) fifth and Chris Fargher (Yamaha) sixth. Cannell dropped to seventh, and sadly Gene McDonnell suffered fatal injuries in a freak accident when he collided with a loose horse on the approach to Ballaugh.

On lap four Steve Cull took over at the front from Mellor and Leach, with the former leader Padgett dropping to fourth, Cannell and Weeden completed the leaderboard. Lap five saw Leach in second place ahead of Mellor, and Padgett dropped to seventh.

Steve Cull won his second race on the T.T. Course by just under a minute from Mellor, Cannell, Leach, Weeden and Padgett.

Third place finisher Graham Cannell at Ballacraine.

Left arm raised in triumph - Roger Burnett sees the welcome sight of the chequered flag

1986 Senior T.T. (six laps - 226.38 miles)

Roger Burnett   500 Honda   113.98 mph

The Senior race was started by the Guest of Honour, His Royal Highness the Duke of Kent.

Roger Marshall (Honda) set the pace from the start and led Trevor Nation (Suzuki) by just 0.8 seconds at the end of the opening lap. Joey Dunlop, Roger Burnett and Geoff Johnson, all Hondas, were next with sixth place being held by Barry Woodland (Suzuki). Nation set the fastest lap of the race on lap two and took the lead from Marshall by 2.2 seconds, Burnett moved ahead of Dunlop.

At half distance, Nation's lead over Marshall was 3.6 seconds and Dunlop was again ahead of Burnett. But Trevor Nation went out on lap four, out of fuel at the 32nd milestone - Marshall was back in front by 11 seconds from Burnett and Dunlop. But two of the leaders had problems in the pits, Marshall lost time when his chain needed adjustments and Dunlop lost three minutes with steering damper problems.

So Roger Burnett took advantage of the mishaps, grabbed the lead and went on to win his first T.T. at 113.98 mph from Geoff Johnson, Barry Woodland, Joey Dunlop, Phil Mellor and Roger Marshall.

Geoff Johnson on the ex-Wayne Gardner 750cc Honda.

Luckless Roger Marshall.

Joey at Parliament Square, Ramsey

1987 Formula One (six laps - 226.38 miles)

Joey Dunlop
750 Honda
115.03 mph (record)

Joey Dunlop duly won his fifth Formula 1 race in succession, but got a shock at his signalling station near Kirk Michael on the first lap when it read - 3!

He turned on the power and led at the end of the opening lap by 21 seconds from the early leader Phil Mellor (Suzuki) with Roger Marshall (Suzuki) in third place 2.8 seconds down. They were followed by Geoff Johnson (Yamaha), Andy McGladdery (Suzuki) and Nick Jefferies (Honda).

With a new lap record on lap two at 117.55 mph he increased his lead to 25.4 seconds from Mellor - Johnson took third place from Marshall, and Jefferies moved ahead of McGladdery.

The top five remained the same at half distance, Joey increased his lead to 26 seconds, but Andy McGladdery retired at Ballaugh Bridge bringing Trevor Nation (Yamaha) into sixth place. The top three maintained their positions to the flag, and on lap four Nation took fourth place from Marshall who appeared to be suffering from fuel starvation.

But Marshall was back in fourth place by the end of lap five with Nation just a couple of seconds ahead of Jefferies.

Joey won from Phil by 51.8 seconds at a new record speed of 115.03 mph and the top six finished in the order that they had started the final lap.

Resilient Nick Jefferies took sixth place.

Joey Dunlop watches as final preparations are made to his Rothmans Honda prior to the win number five in the Formula 1 race. Mechanics Nick Goodison (left) and Peter McNab are still involved with Honda's racing activities.

1987 Senior T.T. (four laps - 150.92 miles)

Joey Dunlop   750 Honda   99.85 mph

The Senior race was delayed to the Saturday because of inclement weather, and even then it was reduced to four laps. Conditions can be judged by the fact that Joey's opening lap was at 105.08 mph - and he led Suzuki-mounted Phil Mellor by 15.6 seconds.

Trevor Nation had his Suzuki in third place six seconds down and was followed by Roger Marshall (Suzuki), Andy McGladdery (Suzuki) and Geoff Johnson (Yamaha). The weather worsened and Joey completed his second lap at 98.64 mph as Phil Mellor closed the gap to just under 10 seconds. Johnson jumped from sixth to third place with Nation fourth, Marshall fifth and McGladdery sixth.

Lap speeds continued to drop on lap three - Joey did 96.79 mph and led Mellor by 27 seconds - Phil had slid off at the Nook, quickly remounted but was forced to retire at the pits with an injured shoulder. So Joey won at an average speed of 99.85 mph - the slowest Senior since 1974 - from Geoff Johnson by 58 seconds with Roger Marshall in third place. McGladdery took fourth, Nick Jefferies brought his Honda into fifth place and Nation finished sixth.

Joey said afterwards that he would never race in conditions like that again. It was his 10th win - bringing him level with Stanley Woods and Giacomo Agostini.

above: Joey takes a cautious line through the puddles at Quarter Bridge before (left) squirting his two-stroke 500cc Honda along to Braddan Bridge and win number 10

Brian Morrison - tight in at Sulby Bridge

1988 Production C (four laps - 150.92 miles)

Brian Morrison   **600 Honda**   **108.42 mph** (record)

Increased to four laps and held on the Friday evening, - this race was a real cracker - the lap record being bettered no fewer than 73 times!!

Roger Hurst (Kawasaki) led at the end of the first lap by 10 seconds, chased by a pack of five Honda riders who were separated by just four seconds - Brian Morrison, Alan Batson, Steve Hislop, Steve Ward and Dave Leach. The top six remained unchanged at the end of the second lap and Hurst held a seven second advantage over Morrison.

There were changes to the top six after lap three - Hurst still led from Morrison but by just 1.4 seconds, Leach was third, Hislop fourth, Ward fifth and Batson sixth. So to the final lap, Brian Morrison lapped at 109.82 mph and snatched a dramatic victory from Roger Hurst by three seconds. Steve Hislop, with the fastest lap of the race at 109.83 mph, a new record, took third ahead of Dave Leach, Steve Ward and Alan Batson.

Alan Batson kerb-skims at Greeba Castle on his way to sixth place.

With a maiden T.T. victory in sight - Steve Hislop cranks the RC30 into the Bungalow

1988 Production B (four laps - 150.92 miles)

Steve Hislop   750 Honda   112.29 mph (record)

A Scottish battle in the Saturday afternoon sunshine between Steve Hislop and Brian Morrison on their 750 Hondas delighted the crowds throughout the four laps - and they had to stop at the end of each lap for fuel.

The opening lap saw Hislop with the advantage by 1.2 seconds. Geoff Johnson (Yamaha) was third ahead of Joey Dunlop (Honda), Jamie Whitham (Suzuki) and Nick Jefferies (Honda). Morrison opened the taps on lap two and with a lap at 111.73 mph led Hislop by 2.8 seconds - Johnson remained third but Whitham took fourth place from Dunlop and Kevin Wilson (Suzuki) took over sixth with Jefferies dropping to seventh.

The boot was on the other foot after three laps had been completed - Steve led Brian by 11 seconds and Johnson hung on in there in third - Dunlop was back in front of Whitham

and Jefferies regained sixth place from Wilson. On the final lap Brian Morrison tried all he knew to catch Hislop - he was just three seconds down at the Bungalow, but he started to suffer from a lack of fuel and spluttered in to finish second - 12.4 seconds down on Steve.

Geoff Johnson took third, Jamie Whitham fourth ahead of Joey Dunlop and Nick Jefferies.

Joey Dunlop, an unaccustomed fifth place

Visor manufacturer and Mountain master - Bob Heath

Six in a row for Joey - first time ever achieved

1988 Formula 1 (six laps - 226.38 miles)

Joey Dunlop **750 Honda** **116.25 mph** (record)

This year the Formula 1 race did not open the meeting, it was transferred to the Monday - but it made no difference to Joey who made it six in a row.

With an opening lap at 116.77 mph he led fellow Honda rider Nick Jefferies by 14 seconds with Yamaha-mounted Geoff Johnson in third place just 0.8 seconds down. The first lap leaderboard was completed by Roger Hurst (Kawasaki), Phil Mellor (Suzuki) and Roger Burnett (Honda).

Joey set a new lap record second time around - 118.54 mph - and led by 29 seconds, but from Johnson who now led Jefferies by 3.4 seconds. Steve Hislop (Honda), seventh on lap one shot up to fourth place with a lap just one second slower than Joey's new record, Hurst dropped to fifth and Paul Iddon (Yamaha) took sixth place. Phil Mellor had retired and Roger Burnett arrived at the pit in 10th place - having ridden with a rear wheel puncture from Ballacraine!!

Lap three saw Joey leading by 26.8 seconds, but from Hislop, now six seconds up on Johnson. Jefferies was fourth, Iddon fifth and Carl Fogarty (Honda) came up to sixth - Roger Hurst having come off at Brandish without injury. No change to the top six after lap four - but Hislop had taken 7.8 seconds off Dunlop's lead. Sadly, Steve Hislop's challenge ended at Bishopscourt on lap five, so Joey was 41 seconds up on Johnson with Jefferies third and Burnett came back on the leaderboard in sixth place.

Next of the leaders to go was Johnson - out at Ballacraine with an oil leak - so Honda riders filled the first four places, Dunlop, Jefferies, Burnett and Fogarty with Iddon fifth and Mark Farmer (Suzuki) grabbed the final leaderboard place.

Roger Burnett eases out of the saddle to let the mechanic fit the stand to change the punctured rear wheel. Leaving his adjacent pit is Robert Dunlop

Win number two this week for Joey - here on song at the Guthrie Memorial

1988 Junior T.T. (four laps - 150.92 miles)

Joey Dunlop   **250 Honda**   **111.87 mph** (record)

The four-lap Junior race included a class for Formula 2 machines - the Junior was for 201 - 350 cc capacities and the F2 for 400-600cc four strokes.

Joey set off at his usual pace and led at the end of the opening lap by 12 seconds from Brian Reid on the E.M.C. who in turn had a 15-second advantage over Ian Young on the 600 Honda. Eddie Laycock (E.M.C.), Brian Morrison (600 Honda) and Johnny Rea (347 Yamaha) completed the top six.

Joey increased his lead to 20 seconds at half distance and surprisingly the top six stayed the same. But Joey had a problem at his pit stop - the petrol cap fell into the fairing, Joey leapt of the machine and his crew tilted the bike to retrieve it - but going down Bray he noticed that it was loose and rode one-handed until he could fasten it properly.

This obviously cost him time and when the third lap times were posted, he was just four seconds ahead with a lap to go. Laycock took over third place followed by Young, Morrison and Rea. Joey made no mistake on the final lap - he increased his lead at the flag to 20 seconds from Brian while Eddie Laycock remained in third place.

The first Formula 2 machine home was the 600 Honda of Brian Morrison in fourth place, Rea finished fifth and Steve Cull on a 250 Honda took sixth place - Ian Young had a slow last lap and finished 10th.

Steve Cull heads for sixth.

Brian Morrison - first Formula Two rider home.

A second T.T. week hat-trick of wins for Joey - 'Yer Maun' head into Braddan Bridge.

1988 Senior T.T. (six laps - 226.38 miles)

Joey Dunlop   748 Honda   117.38 mph (record)

Joey duly completed another hat-trick of wins with a record-breaking ride in the six-lap Senior T.T. After lap one he led on his 748 Honda by 5.2 seconds from Steve Cull on the 500 Honda, who was six seconds ahead of Nick Jefferies (748 Honda). Roger Marshall (Suzuki) held fourth, Roger Burnett (Honda) was fifth with Phil Mellor (Suzuki) completing the top six, and amazingly 104 riders completed the first lap.

Cull really flew on the second lap and set a new lap record at 119.08 mph, closing to within 1.4 seconds of the leader. Nick Jefferies went out at Union Mills so Marshall took over third place - Steve Hislop (748 Honda), eighth at the end of the first lap shot up to fourth place with Burnett fifth and Geoff Johnson

(750 Yamaha) sixth - Mellor dropped to seventh.

At half distance Joey was just 4.4 seconds in front of Cull - Hislop was now up to third ahead of Mellor, Marshall was fifth and Johnson sixth with Burnett seventh. Lap four saw Joey leading by 42 seconds from Hislop with Cull third followed by Johnson, Burnett and Marshall. Steve Cull's problem was a holed expansion chamber - attempts to repair it at the pits failed and he carried on but was down on power. Joey was now in command, at the end of lap five he was almost a minute ahead of Hislop, Johnson took third place from a slowing Cull and Burnett and Marshall stayed in the top six.

But Steve Cull's luck ran out on the last lap when his machine caught fire on the descent from the Creg. Joey won from Steve with Johnson third, Marshall took fourth place ahead of Burnett and Brian Morrison (750 Honda). Of the 104 riders who completed lap one, 68 of them made it to the flag.

Steve Cull, on the ex-Joey Dunlop NS500, pictured here approaching Brandywell.

1984 Senior Manx Grand Prix winner Dave Pither at Windy Corner.

First Supersport 600 winner Steve Hislop on a lonely Mountain road at Keppel Gate

1989 Supersport 600 (four laps - 150.92 miles)

Steve Hislop   600 Honda   112.58 mph (record)

A Supersport 600 race was introduced to the programme for 1989 and held over four laps of the course.

Steve Hislop opened with a lap at 113.15 mph to lead Dave Leach (Yamaha) by 14.6 seconds with the Suzukis of Phil Mellor and James Whitham third and fourth followed by Nick Jefferies (Yamaha) and Brian Morrison (Honda).

With the fastest lap of the race second time around - 113.60 mph - Leach knocked 0.2 seconds of Steve's lead, Whitham took third place from Mellor and Jefferies and Morrison retained their leaderboard places.

Steve opened the taps on lap three and pulled out a 27.2 second lead over Leach and the only change to the top six was that Morrison took fifth place from Jefferies.

Steve Hislop closed with a lap at 112.66 mph and extended his lead over Dave at the flag to 28.8 seconds - the relia-bility of these machines was proved when the leaderboard remained unchanged.

Even before he removes his helmet at the end, Steve Hislop wants essential information from his Honda team.

Brian Morrison at Parliament Square.

Steve Hislop gives Honda their 11th Formula One win

1989 Formula 1 (six laps - 226.38 miles)

Steve Hislop   750 Honda   119.36 mph (record)

With Joey Dunlop out of the T.T. due to an injury sustained at Brands Hatch - who would take over the mantle of T.T. F1 winner? Would the first 120+ lap be recorded? Questions that didn't take long to answer.

Steve Hislop opened with a lap in 19m. 43.2s - a speed of 120.92 to lead fellow Honda rider Brian Morrison by 26.2 seconds with the Yamaha of Nick Jefferies in third place. Carl Fogarty (Honda), Steve Cull (Norton) and Jamie Whitham (Suzuki) made up the leaderboard.

Steve increased the lap record to 121.34 mph on lap two and led by 38 seconds from Morrison with Jefferies still third. Fogarty remained fourth, Robert Dunlop (Honda) jumped up to fifth with Cull sixth and Whitham just off the leaderboard in seventh place. The top three remained the same at half distance - but Whitham was back up to fourth, Fogarty was fifth and Graeme McGregor (750 Honda), who had started at No. 32 came up to sixth with Dunlop seventh and Cull 10th.

No changes at all to the top six on lap four and Hislop was leading one minute 13 seconds. But Steve Cull's race ended in retirement at Creg-ny-Baa. Lap five changes saw Fogarty up to fourth ahead of McGregor and Whitham. The order stayed like that to the finish and Hislop, Morrison and Fogarty gave Honda the Manufacturers award; 10 of the top 12 finishers were on Hondas.

Tidy boots - tidy style - Carl Fogarty at Quarter Bridge

Slick pit work in the Brian Morrison camp

More at home on the 750 - Carl Fogarty prepares for the Mountain climb

1989 Production 750 (four laps - 15.92 miles)

Carl Fogarty   750 Honda   114.68 mph   (record)

Steve Hislop was the firm favourite to take this four lap race, but pitted for fuel after each lap - Carl Fogarty opted to go for the first two laps non-stop - throw in Dave Leach on a very fast Yamaha, and you had all the ingredients for a first class race.

At the end of the opening lap Steve had the lead, but by just 1.6 seconds from Dave with Carl 4.4 seconds back in third. Nick Jefferies had his Yamaha in fourth place followed by the Hondas of Brian Morrison and Bob Jackson.

Fogarty's tactics seemed to be working as by half distance he had grabbed the lead by three seconds from Leach with

Hislop now third and the rest of the top six the same. Hislop fought back on the third lap and took second place from Leach by 13 seconds, and was 8.8 seconds down on Fogarty.

Tremendous excitement on the final lap - the top three were almost side by side around the course - at the Creg Fogarty and Leach were together with Hislop keeping a watching brief some yards back. The charge was on to the flag - Fogarty or Leach - who would it be? Carl grabbed it by 1.4 seconds, despite Dave setting a new lap record - Steve took a safe third place - a brilliant ride considering he had stopped for fuel three times in the race. Nick Jefferies finished fourth, Brian Morrison fifth and Ian Young (Honda) pipped Bob Jackson for sixth place.

Bob Jackson, had to settle for seventh.

Steve Hislop gives the crowd a close-up at the Gooseneck on his way to third place..

Dunlop Junior - Robert at Ramsey

1989 Ultra Lightweight T.T. (two laps - 75.46 miles)

Robert Dunlop   125 Honda   102.58 mph (record)

The return of the little 125cc machines attracted an excellent entry, but the race distance was just two laps - a real sprint.

Robert Dunlop set a new lap record from a standing start at 102.15 mph and led Ian Lougher by 9.4 seconds. Ian in turn was 15 seconds ahead of Ian Newton, and all three had lapped at over the ton. The top six was completed by Carl Fogarty, Michael McGarrity and Richard Swallow - all on Hondas, as were 23 of the 30 riders who completed the first lap. With a new lap record at 103.02 mph on the final lap, Robert won by 15.8 seconds from Ian Lougher. Carl Fogarty took third place from Ian Newton while Mick McGarrity and Richard Swallow finished fifth and sixth respectively.

A new name - Phillip McCallen - took seventh place - he had won the 1988 Manx Grand Prix Newcomers 250cc and Lightweight Races.

Carl Fogarty on the only 125 outing of his illustrious career.

Can you guess where this was taken? An unusual angle as Steve Hislop leaves Ballaugh Bridge and exits the village

1989 Senior T.T. (six laps - 226.38 miles)

Steve Hislop   **750 Honda**   **118.23 mph** (record)

Steve Hislop had the chance to join Mike Hailwood and Joey Dunlop in the hat-trick club - and he made no mistakes in the final race of the week. He blasted off from the line and returned 18m. 50.4s later - 120.15 mph - to lead Yamaha's Nick Jefferies by 21.6 seconds.

Trevor Nation had the 588 Norton in third place, just ahead of Carl Fogarty (Honda). Graeme McGregor (Honda) and Dave Leach (Yamaha) completed the first lap leaderboard. Steve set a new lap record next time around - 120.69 mph - to add another eight seconds to his lead. McGregor moved up to third ahead of Fogarty, Nation dropped to fifth and Leach remained in sixth place.

Half distance saw the top four unchanged - and Steve's lead was up to 35 seconds. Leach was fifth and Nation now sixth. The only change to the leaderboard after the fourth lap times had been posted was that Robert Dunlop brought his

Honda into sixth place. Dave Leach had been black-flagged because of a loose fairing - he tied it on and proceeded but dropped to 16th place.

There were changes on lap five - but not affecting the first three. Carl Fogarty retired at the pits with an oil leak and Trevor Nation went out at Crosby with waterpump failure. So Robert Dunlop moved up to fourth and Andy McGladdery and Eddie Laycock brought their Hondas on to the leaderboard. Steve went on to complete his hat-trick by 38 seconds at a new race record speed from Jefferies, McGregor, Dunlop, and Laycock took fifth place from McGladdery.

The Mayor of Douglas, Freddie Kennish presents Steve with the Jimmy Simpson Trophy, for the fastest lap of the meeting; both Jimmy and Steve came from Hawick, on the Scottish borders.

Andy McGladdery aviates at Ballaugh Bridge heading for sixth place on Francis Neill's RC30.

The Waterworks holds no fear for rampant Fogarty

1990 Formula 1 (six laps - 226.38 miles)

Carl Fogarty   **750 Honda**   **118.35 mph**

Carl Fogarty opened proceedings with a lap at 120.50 mph to lead Nick Jefferies (Yamaha) by 21.6 seconds with Robert Dunlop on the 588 Norton in third place just 2.4 seconds down.

The Hondas of Ian Young and Brian Morrison and the Norton of Trevor Nation completed the first lap top six. Joey Dunlop was back, although not 100% fit and held 10th place. The drama happened early however when hot favourite Steve Hislop suffered brake problems on the opening lap and was in 20th place. Fogarty still led at the end of lap two, but from Robert Dunlop by 40 seconds, Jefferies was third, Morrison fourth, Nation fifth and with the retirement of Ian Young, Dave Leach brought his Yamaha into sixth place.

Joey was ninth and after a long pit stop Steve was in 39th place. At half distance, Fogarty was ahead of Jefferies who had retaken second place from Robert Dunlop with the rest of the top six the same. Joey was still ninth and Steve shot up to 27th.

There were no changes to the leaderboard after lap four, and Carl had a lead of 50 seconds. With a lap at 121.99 mph Hislop was up to 18th. On lap five Leach moved up to fifth place, Graeme McGregor brought his

Honda into sixth place with Nation down to seventh. Hislop was now in 13th place. The final lap saw only one change to the top six, when Trevor Nation regained sixth place from McGregor.

Carl Fogarty won by 51.2 seconds from Nick Jefferies, and with a new lap record on the final lap at 122.63 mph, Steve Hislop took eighth place, just one ahead of Joey Dunlop. Hislop, Fogarty and Joey gave Honda the Manufacturers award.

It's only one-man, Ernie Coates power for Joey's RC30 out of the pits after refuelling. The single-sided swing arm makes for rapid wheel changes, which take less time than a refuel

Robert 'Micro' Dunlop takes 125 win number two

1990 Ultra Lightweight T.T. (three laps - 113.19 miles)

Robert Dunlop   125 Honda   103.41 mph (record)

The 125cc race distance was increased to three laps for 1990, and Honda totally dominated the race.

Robert Dunlop was all out to repeat his 1989 success, and led at the end of the opening lap by 7.6 seconds from Ian Newton with Joey Dunlop in third place, 14 seconds adrift. Michael Topping, 'Bud' Jackson and Alan Caughey made up the leaderboard - all on Hondas.

Robert set a new lap record on lap two - 104.09 mph - and led Ian by 19 seconds with Joey still third. The only change was that Caughey took fifth place from Jackson.

With the first two setting identical times on the last lap, Robert Dunlop took a record-breaking win by 19.6 seconds from Ian Newton. But Joey's luck ran out with retirement at Douglas Road Corner, Kirk Michael, so Michael Topping took third place. Caughey, Jackson and Aubrey McCauley completed the leaderboard.

Of the 33 finishers - 32 rode Hondas!!

Skelmersdale's Ian Newton keeps the 'wheels down' at Ballaugh Bridge.

Michael Topping gets his 125 on the tight line at Braddan Bridge.

Senior victory and a 750 double for Carl Fogarty

1990 Senior T.T. (six laps - 226.38 miles)

Carl Fogarty   750 Honda   110.95 mph

Due to the weather conditions the race was postponed from 11 a.m. to 4.30 p.m. and even then they were far from ideal for the 1990 Senior - a fact that can be seen from the first lap times - Carl Fogarty led with a lap at 108.52 mph by 21.4 seconds from Trevor Nation (Norton) with Phillip McCallen (Honda) in third place a further 5.4 seconds down.

He was followed by Steve Ward (Honda), Robert Dunlop (Norton) and Dave Leach (Yamaha). Steve Hislop held 12th place and Joey was 22nd. McCallen took over second place at the end of lap two from Nation with the other riders in the same places as lap one.

At half distance Fogarty led from Nation by almost a minute with McCallen in third place. Dave Leach jumped up to fourth ahead of Ward and Robert Dunlop, but Steve Hislop's race ended in retirement at the pits. By the time lap four

had been completed Dave Leach was up to third place behind Fogarty and Nation, with Ward fourth, Robert Dunlop fifth and Brian Morrison (Honda) came on to the leaderboard after Phillip McCallen retired after a spill at the Nook. Next of the leaderboard men to retire was Robert Dunlop, his Norton caught fire at Kirk Michael, so Steve Williams (Yamaha) took over sixth place.

Carl Fogarty completed his 1990 750cc double by one minute 18.8 seconds from Trevor Nation with Dave Leach third, then came Steve Ward, Brian Morrison and Steve Williams. Joey took a bronze replica for 16th place.

Steve Ward on Union Mills Bridge heads for fourth.

Slicks are not the ideal choice for a rain soaked road; Eddie Laycock treads warily round Quarter Bridge.

Where's Foggy? Steve Hislop glances back to check where his early shadow had got to

1991 Formula 1 (six laps - 226.38 miles)

Steve Hislop   750 Honda   121.00 mph

After his disappointments of 1990, Steve was in a determined mood - in practice he had lapped at 124.36 mph - the fastest ever lap recorded - and Joey Dunlop had recorded his first ever 120 plus lap.

The opening lap saw Hislop, with a lap at 122.83 mph, in the lead by 9.4 seconds from team-mate Carl Fogarty with Brian Morrison (Yamaha) in third place, 9.8 seconds down. Trevor Nation (Norton), Dave Leach (Yamaha) and Robert Dunlop (Norton) completed the top six. Joey limped in to the pits in 21st place after a fork seal broke and he retired.

By the time the second lap had been completed - Steve went round at a new course record speed of 123.48 mph - he was 30 seconds ahead of Carl and the only change to the leaderboard was that Phillip McCallen (Honda) took fifth place, Leach was sixth and Robert Dunlop was eighth, but he retired because of his injured collarbone.

The top three were the same at half distance. McCallen was up to fourth ahead of Nation and Steve Cull (Honda) - Dave Leach retired at the pits. Hislop was 31 seconds ahead of Fogarty after four laps with Morrison over a minute down in third place - Nation was back up to fourth being chased by McCallen and Cull.

The gap at the front was 38.2 seconds after five laps had been completed, Nation was third followed by McCallen, Morrison and Cull, but Cull's race ended with a retirement at the pits.

Steve Hislop won by one minute 16 seconds from Carl Fogarty, Trevor Nation finished third but was later excluded for an oversize tank, bringing Morrison into the top three, McCallen finished fourth and the top six was completed by Steve Ward (Honda) and Bob Jackson (Honda).

The Honda "B" Team of Nick Jefferies (8th), Phillip McCallen (5th) and Johnny Rea (13th) took the Manufacturers award.

The Honda team were out for a video session in Friday evening practice. The forward-facing camera on Nick Jefferies RC30 (7) gave trouble early on, and the rear-facing one on Carl Fogarty's bike probably only showed the road, judging by this Lambfell shot! Steve Hislop is in close attendance.

Dave Wells helps Mick Boddice to keep an even keel over Ballaugh Bridge

1991 Sidecar T.T. 'A' (three laps - 113.19 miles)

Mick Boddice/Dave Wells   600 Honda   99.26 mph

Mick and Dave gave Honda their first ever Sidecar victory with a start to finish win.

At the end of the first lap they led Geoff Bell / Keith Cornbill (Yamaha) by 4.4 seconds with Neil Smith / Steve Mace (350 Yamaha) third a further 8.6 seconds down. Gordon Shand / Nicholas Kay (600 Shand), Roy and Tom Hanks (350 NRTH Ireson) and Artie Oates / Stuart Pitts (600 Kawasaki) made up the first lap leaderboard.

At the end of lap two Mick's lead was 20.6 seconds, due to the fastest lap of the race at 99.85 mph, but now from Smith who had overtaken Bell. Oates moved up to fourth, Hanks remained fifth and Eddy Wright / Andy Hetherington (350 Shellbourne) took sixth place, the Shand outfit having retired at Churchtown, Lezayre. Mick and Dave went on to win from Smith and Mace by 16 seconds.

Oates and Pitts took over third place followed by Wright / Hetherington, Roy and Tom Hanks and Geoff Bell / Keith Cornbill - who had been reported as touring at Hillberry - came in sixth.

The traffic mirror shows that Allan Shand and Neill Miller have a clear run up through White Gates.

At Ginger Hall - Robert on his way to a hat-trick of 125 wins

1991 Ultra Lightweight T.T. (four laps - 150.92 miles)

Robert Dunlop   125 Honda   103.68 mph (record)

Robert Dunlop scored his third successive record-breaking win in the 125cc race, increased in distance this year to four laps.

But it was big brother Joey who led at the end of the first lap by 22 seconds with Phillip McCallen a further 6.4 seconds down in third place. Bob Heath, Stan Rea and Steve Ward, all on Hondas, made up the top six.

At the half-distance pit stops, Joey led his brother by 19.8 seconds and the rest of the top six was unchanged. But Joey had a problem. A slow pit stop in which the petrol breather pipe was broken robbed him of his 14th T.T. win.

Yet at the end of the third lap he was only 4.4 seconds down on Robert - Heath and McCallen were tied for third place followed by Bob Jackson and and Steve Ward - Stan

Rea having retired at Governors Bridge.

Robert got the message however, and with a new lap record at 106.71 mph he took the chequered flag to complete a hat-trick of wins, Joey was second, Bob Heath took third with Phillip McCallen, Bob Jackson and Steve Ward completing the top six. There were 33 finishers - and all were on Hondas.

The Dunlop brothers and Phillip McCallen gave Honda another Manufacturers award.

Joey Dunlop takes the Andy McMenemy RS 125 across the Mountain in pursuit of brother Robert and victory.

Bob Heath makes the little 125 work hard up the Mountain at the Guthrie Memorial.

On their way to a sidecar double, Mick and Dave climb aboard

1991 Sidecar T.T. 'B' (three laps - 113.19 miles)

Mick Boddice/Dave Wells   600 Honda   99.27 mph

Mick Boddice completed the double for Honda and notched up his ninth sidecar T.T. victory, equalling the record of Siegfried Schauzu and Dave Saville.

With Dave Wells again in the chair he led the Bell / Cornbill outfit at the end of the opening lap by 11.4 seconds with Roy and Tom Hanks in third place just 2.6 seconds down. Kenny Howles / Alan Langton (350 Ireson), Dave Molyneux / Karl Ellison (600 Kawasaki) and John Holden / Ian Watson (600 Kawasaki) completed the top six.

With a lap at 100.15 mph second time around, Mick increased his lead over Geoff to 44.4 seconds and Howles moved up to third ahead of Molyneux. Holden was fifth and Eddy Wright / Andy Hetherington were sixth - the Hanks outfit having retired at Handley's Corner.

Mick won the race by 32.2 seconds from Geoff, Molyneux regained third place from Howles, Holden was fifth and the Oates / Pitts outfit took sixth spot. Wright and Hetherington hit problems on the last lap and in fact pushed in from Governors Bridge to take a bronze replica for 17th place.

Duncan Burns fails to keep the sidecar wheel down as Joseph Heys barrels through Union Mills.

Steve Hislop is already ahead of Brian Morrison and Joey Dunlop at the Bungalow

1991 Supersport 600 (four laps - 150.92 miles)

Steve Hislop   600 Honda   114.28 mph   (record)

Dave Leach (Yamaha) was all fired up for a Supersport double, but Steve Hislop had other ideas.

At the end of the lap it was the Honda rider in front, but by just 1.2 seconds, with Bob Jackson's Honda in third place, 1.8s down on Leach. Steve Ives (Yamaha), Steve Cull (Yamaha) and Brian Morrison (Yamaha) made up the first lap top six.

With a new lap record second time round at 115.69 mph, Hislop increased his lead over Leach to 8.6 seconds, Cull had taken third place with Jackson fourth, Morrison fifth and Ives sixth.

The race was in Steve's pocket after three laps when he led Cull by 34.8 seconds Jackson was third, Dave Leach fourth but he retired at the pits, Ives was fifth and Phillip McCallen (Honda) took sixth place.

Steve won his second race of the week by 30 seconds from Steve Cull, Bob Jackson retained his third place, Steve Ives took fourth ahead of Phillip McCallen and Joey Dunlop (Honda) took sixth place.

Dunlop, Hislop and McCallen took the Manufacturers award.

Racer-journalist Ray Knight at Parliament Square. Later that year, he took the race plates off, fitted panniers and took the wife for a touring holiday round the Pyrenees on his CBR600!

Bob Jackson rounds Ballacraine on his way to third place.

Steve Hislop scored his second T.T. week hat-trick in the Senior

1991 Senior T.T. (six laps - 226.38 miles)

Steve Hislop
750 Honda
121.09 mph (record)

With the fastest ever race average speed, Steve Hislop led the Senior from start to finish and notched up his second hat-trick of T.T. wins, equalling the record of Mike Hailwood and Joey Dunlop.

His opening lap at 121.09 mph put him 9.8 seconds ahead of Joey Dunlop who had taken over Carl Fogarty's works RVF Honda for the Senior. Trevor Nation had his Norton in third place 8.2 seconds down on Joey, with Brian Morrison (Yamaha), Phillip McCallen (Honda) and Dave Leach (Yamaha) completing the top six. Steve increased his lead over Joey to 18.8 seconds after lap two and the only change to the leaderboard was that Morrison took third place from Nation.

At half distance the gap between first and second was up to 29 seconds, Morrison was still third, McCallen fourth, Nick Jefferies (Honda) fifth and Steve Linsdell (Yamaha) sixth - Trevor Nation had retired with a seized engine at the Bungalow and Dave Leach dropped to ninth. Lap four saw Hislop 49.8 seconds ahead of Dunlop, third to fifth remained the same, but Bob Jackson (Honda) took sixth place when Steve Linsdell hit problems and a lap at 89 mph dropped him to 18th place.

By the time lap five had been completed Hislop had a 64 second advantage, and the question was could he catch his team-mate on the road on the final lap. With a new lap record at 123.27 mph he did and they crossed the line together, to give Steve the win by two minutes 20 seconds, Phillip McCallen moved up to third place to give Honda the Manufacturers award, Brian Morrison took fourth followed by Nick Jefferies and Bob Jackson.

An unusual view of Joey - but not for most of the entry! Joey Dunlop accelerates through Sarah's Cottage and up Creg Willey's Hill.

The Formula One race gave a first T.T. win to Phillip McCallen

1992 Formula 1 (six laps - 226.38 miles)

Phillip McCallen   750 Honda   119.80 mph

Honda, Yamaha and Norton were the top runners in the six-lap opening race of the week.

Lap one saw Carl Fogarty (Yamaha) in front by 11 seconds from Phillip McCallen (Honda) with Norton-mounted Steve Hislop in third place a further 2.8 seconds down. Joey Dunlop had his Honda in fourth place followed by Mark Farmer (Yamaha) and Robert Dunlop (Norton). No change to the top five after two laps, but Nick Jefferies brought his Yamaha into sixth place with the retirement of Robert Dunlop at Kirk Michael with a seized engine.

Half distance, and Fogarty's lead over McCallen was up to 27 seconds with Hislop still third, but now 22 seconds adrift. Jefferies had overtaken Farmer, and that was the only leader-board change. No changes to the top six after four laps, but on the fifth lap Carl Fogarty limped into the pits in sixth place to retire.

So Phillip McCallen took over at the front - 18.8 seconds up on Hislop. Joey moved up to third, Nick Jefferies was fourth, Mark Farmer fifth and with Fogarty's retirement, Steve Ward brought his Honda into sixth place.

Steve Hislop set the fastest lap of the race on the final circuit, but it was not fast enough to stop Phillip McCallen winning his first T.T. Race, and Hondas continuing dominance of the F1 event, and another Manufacturers award with riders Dunlop, Jefferies and McCallen.

Fourth place and member of the winning manufacturers team, Nick Jefferies, seen here at Governors Bridge.

No Limit! Joey wheelies out of Rhencullen.

Win number 14 for 'Yer Maun'

1992 Ultra Lightweight T.T. (four laps - 150.92 miles)

Joey Dunlop   **125 Honda**   **106.49 mph** (record)

Joey finally achieved his ambition of equalling Mike Hailwood's record of 14 T.T. wins, and he did it in record breaking style with a start to finish victory.

Younger brother Robert, winner for the past three years, held second place throughout the four-lap race. After lap one, 3.6 seconds separated the brothers, with Mick Lofthouse in third place 26 seconds back. He was followed by Stephen Johnson, Ian Lougher and Stan Rea - all on Hondas.

Robert was faster on lap two, and trailed Joey by just 0.2 seconds at the pit stops, Lofthouse and Johnson retained their positions, but Rea overtook Lougher and newcomer Denis McCullough was pushing hard in seventh place. Joey increased his speed on the third lap and stretched his lead to 7.6 seconds, and the rest of the leaderboard remained the same.

On the final lap, the Dunlop brothers both lapped at over 108 mph, Robert at 108.62 mph with Joey marginally quicker at 108.69 mph - a new lap record and a victory by 8.4 seconds. Mick Lofthouse held his third place, Stan Rea was fourth, Stephen Johnson fifth and Denis McCullough snatched sixth place from Ian Lougher by three seconds.

The Honda "B" team of Richard Coates (20th), Ian Lougher (7th) and Bob Jackson (13th) won the Manufacturers award - there were 37 finishers and all rode Hondas.

Ian Lougher leads Mark Westmoreland into Sulby Bridge, after the flat-out Sulby Straight

Another 1 - 2 - 3 for Honda

1992 Supersport 600 (four laps - 150.92 miles)

Phillip McCallen   600 Honda   115.04 mph (record)

This four-lap race gave Phillip McCallen his second win of the week, despite a strong late challenge from Steve Hislop.

At the end of lap one McCallen led Bob Jackson (Honda) by 12 seconds with the Yamaha of Johnny Rea in third place five seconds back. The Hondas of Steve Hislop, Steve Ward and Nick Jefferies made up the first lap leaderboard.

Lap two saw McCallen 26.8 seconds in front of Jackson, but Ward jumped to third place, Hislop was still fourth, Rea down to fifth and Jefferies still sixth.

Phillip just got on with the job in hand, whoever was chasing him. After three laps he was 41.2 seconds ahead - but now from Hislop with Ward third and the rest of the top six read: Jefferies, Jackson and Rea.

Steve Hislop set a new lap record on the final circuit at 117.01 mph, but Phillip took the trophy at a record 115.04 mph by 22.8 seconds with the remaining top six places unchanged.

Honda's 'A' team of Joey Dunlop (9th), Phillip McCallen (1st) and Steve Hislop (2nd) earned the Manufacturers award.

Phillip McCallen at Rhencullen

A popular winner - Nick Jefferies at Sulby Bridge

1993 Formula 1 (six laps - 226.38 miles)

Nick Jefferies   750 Honda   118.15 mph

Phillip McCallen with the RVF Honda had been fastest in practice, despite the shoulder injury sustained in the North-West 200. But at the end of the opening lap of the race it was Mark Farmer on the Oxford Ducati that led by three seconds from Nick Jefferies (Honda) with Phillip in third place five seconds down on Jefferies - Robert Dunlop (Ducati) and the Hondas of Steve Ward and Jason Griffiths completed the leaderboard.

Farmer struck trouble on the second lap and came into the pits with rear sprocket problems and retired. The new leader was Jefferies but Ward leapt from fifth to second - 0.2 seconds up on McCallen, Griffiths was fifth and Simon Beck (Honda) took sixth place - Robert Dunlop had run out of petrol and pushed in for 14th place.

By the time half the race distance had been completed Nick Jefferies had a seven-second lead over Phillip McCallen, and

Steve Ward was now third. Griffiths moved up to fourth, Trevor Nation (Yamaha) took fifth place and Johnny Rea brought his Yamaha on to the leaderboard in sixth place - Beck dropping to 11th.

Lap four saw no changes to the top five but Jim Moodie (Honda) climbed to sixth ahead of Rea while Robert Dunlop retired at the pits, feeling the effects of a Friday evening practice spill. There was no drama on the final lap, and Nick Jefferies was a popular winner by 15.2 seconds from McCallen with another fine ride from Steve Ward giving him third place.

Incidentally, this win gave Nick Jefferies a unique record - the only rider to win a T.T., a Manx Grand Prix and the Manx National Two-Day Trial!

With a 1-2-3 finish, Honda took the Manufacturers award.

Privateer Steve Ward added to his T.T. silverware with a fine third place, seen here rounding Governors Bridge.

Phillip McCallen appears to have the Michelin spirit riding with him as he takes Ballacraine.

The masterful Joey Dunlop - now 15 T.T. wins

1993 Ultra Lightweight T.T. (four laps - 150.92 miles)

Joey Dunlop   125 Honda   107.26 mph (record)

Joey rewrote the record books in the four-lap 125cc race, he won with a new race record and notched up his 15th T.T. win - an all time record.

It was the 'Dunlop Brothers' Show' again as they were first and second throughout the 150-mile race, and amazingly the top three remained the same for four laps, with Bob Heath scoring a fine third place.

The opening 37.73 miles saw Joey lapping at 107.25 mph to lead Robert by 7.8 seconds with Bob a further 21.6 seconds down. Chris Fargher, Denis McCullough and Garry Bennett - all Hondas - completed the top six. Chris Fargher retired at Ramsey on lap two so McCullough and Bennett moved up one place and Glen English took sixth place. After the third lap times had been posted it was seen that Joey's advantage was now eight seconds - no change to the top five but Glen English retired at the pits so Richard Parrott moved into the top six.

Joey set the fastest lap of the race on the final circuit - 108.55 mph to win by 12.6 seconds with no other changes, and as last year, all 24 finishers were Honda-mounted. Bob Heath combined with the Dunlop brothers to win the Manufacturers award.

The Dunlop Brothers - a double act that have won the Ultra Lightweight T.T. seven times between them.

Bob Heath rounds Waterworks 2, and lurking in the background is runner-up Robert Dunlop.

Exiting Gooseneck - stylish Scot Jim Moodie

1993 Supersport 600 (four laps - 150.92 miles)

Jim Moodie   600 Honda   115.06 mph (record)

Hondas filled five of the six top places at the end of the first lap, Jim Moodie led by 13.6 seconds from Bob Jackson who was just one second up on Ian Simpson, then came Colin Gable, Mark Farmer (Yamaha) and Nick Jefferies. One of the favourites, Brian Reid retired at the pits in 20th place.

With a new lap record at 116.77 mph, Jim increased his lead to 24.8 seconds at the end of the second circuit, Simon Beck (Honda) jumped on to the leaderboard in fifth place, Farmer was sixth and Jefferies seventh. The only leaderboard man to go out on the third lap was Colin Gable who retired at the pits, the top three remained unchanged with Beck, Farmer and Jefferies in pursuit.

Jim Moodie won by 21.6 seconds from Bob Jackson and with a fast last lap, Simon Beck took third place from Ian Simpson by 1.6 seconds.

The Manufacturers award went to Honda riders Moodie, Jackson and Beck.

Nick Jefferies now says he does not jump Ballaugh Bridge; he certainly did in 1993; note the compression on the rear tyre.

Phillip's first Senior T.T. win came this year

1993 Senior T.T. (six laps - 226.38 miles)

Phillip McCallen   750 Honda   118.32 mph

The Senior race was postponed from the Friday to Saturday because of bad weather, but the 24-hour delay didn't deter Phillip McCallen from notching up his first Senior T.T. victory.

He lapped at over 120 mph from a standing start to lead Mark Farmer's Ducati by 15.8 seconds with Honda riders Joey Dunlop, Nick Jefferies and Simon Beck next and Robert Holden (Yamaha) completed the leaderboard. Mark Farmer retired at Hillberry - out of fuel - on lap two, so Phillip led by 27.4 seconds from Joey with Nick in third place, Steve Ward was fourth, Simon Beck fifth and Jason Griffiths took sixth place - the top six all on Hondas.

The only change to the leaderboard at half-distance was Beck taking fourth place from Ward. Joey had a slight problem with oil on the machine and dropped to fifth at the end of lap four - McCallen led Jefferies by just over one minute, and Ward was still third.

The next of the leaderboard men to retire was Simon Beck at Glen Helen, so after five laps the top six read - McCallen, Jefferies, Ward, Griffiths, Ian Simpson (Kawasaki) and Dunlop.

Phillip McCallen's week ended on a high with victory over Nick Jefferies by 45 seconds, Steve Ward had another fine ride to take third place ahead Jason Griffiths, Ian Simpson and Johnny Rea (Yamaha) who took the final leaderboard place as Joey Dunlop slowed to finish 11th.

The first three riders gave Honda the Manufacturers award once again.

Nick Jefferies at the Bungalow

From a racing family - Jason Griffiths at Quarter Bridge

A sunny Sunday winner - Steve Hislop at Whitegates

1994 Formula 1 (six laps - 226.38 miles)

Steve Hislop 750 Honda 119.54 mph

What a dramatic start to the 1994 Meeting. When riders set off in the Formula 1 race the roads were dry, but by the time they reached Ballacraine the roads were completely wet and the visibility on the Mountain was poor.

Most riders stopped at the end of the first lap to change to wet tyres, but Nigel Davies and Bob Jackson, who had started on non-slick tyres went straight through. Nigel Davies led at 94.65 mph followed by Steve Ward and Bob Jackson all on Hondas. Steve Hislop retired at the pits so on lap two the order was Davies, Jackson and Simon Beck. The race was stopped at the end of the second lap and riders were paid lap money, and the race rescheduled for Sunday.

The weather was fine and Steve Hislop opened with a lap at 121.79 mph to lead Phillip McCallen by 21.8 seconds with Robert Dunlop third 9.6 seconds down. Steve Ward, Joey Dunlop, all on Hondas and Simon Beck (Ducati) completed the top six. Steve increased his lead to 23 seconds on lap two, and Nigel Davies (Honda) came into sixth place with Beck dropping to 13th. No changes to the leaderboard on lap three, but drama struck on lap four, Robert Dunlop crashed heavily on the exit from Ballaugh Bridge due to a rear wheel collapsing, he was flown to hospital with leg and arm injuries. This promoted Steve Ward to third, Joey was fourth, Gary Radcliffe (Honda) was fifth and Davies sixth. On lap five Joey took third place from Ward and Iain Duffus (Yamaha) took over sixth place with Davies dropping to eighth.

Steve won his 10th T.T. Race by 55.2 seconds from Phillip McCallen, who set the fastest lap of the race at 122.08 mph, with Joey Dunlop third, followed by Gary Radcliffe, all Hondas, Iain Duffus (Yamaha) while Nigel Davies (Honda) regained sixth place. Steve Ward hit problems on the last lap and finished 16th.

The treacherous conditions of the curtailed Saturday race are evident as Nigel Davies eases his way through the Bungalow.

Manxman Gary Radcliffe is the latest of a long line of local talent who made their mark on the T.T. races, a Creg ny Baa shot.

On his way to another winner's rostrum - Joey exits Governors Bridge

1994 Ultra Lightweight T.T. (four laps - 150.92 miles)

Joey Dunlop   125 Honda   105.74 mph

Joey took victory number 16 in the 125cc race. After the first of the four laps he led Mick Lofthouse (Yamaha) by 8.6 seconds, with Denis McCullough (Honda) third a further seven seconds down. Ian Lougher had his Aprilia in fourth place, James Courtney (Honda) was fifth and Chris Fargher (Yamaha) sixth. With the fastest lap of the race at 107.40 mph, Joey increased his lead over Lofthouse to 16.6 seconds on lap two and McCullough was still third. But James Courtney retired at Quarter Bridge, Chris Fargher took over fourth place, Glen English (Honda) was fifth and Lougher sixth.

More changes on lap three, Ian Lougher retired and Glen English dropped to eighth - Noel Clegg (Honda) and Gary Dynes (Yamaha) took fifth and sixth places.

Joey went on to win by one minute 11.2 seconds, but from Denis McCullough, Mick Lofthouse having retired at Sulby with a broken exhaust on the last lap. Chris Fargher took third place with Noel Clegg, Glen English and Gary Dynes completing the final leaderboard.

The Manufacturers award went to Honda - riders Dunlop, McCullough and Clegg.

Denis McCullough, another of Francis Neill's aces, takes Ballaugh Bridge.

Chris Fargher achieved his best-ever T.T. placing on the Martin Bullock sponsored 125, pictured here at Sulby Bridge.

Joey on probably the machine he enjoys most, Honda's RS250

1994 Junior T.T. (four laps - 150.92 miles)

Joey Dunlop　　　　　**250 Honda**　　　　　**114.67 mph**

After topping the practice leaderboard, it was no surprise that Phillip McCallen led at the end of the opening lap by 7.6 seconds.

Joey Dunlop was second and Ian Lougher made it a Honda 1-2-3 by holding third place, 4.2 seconds down on Joey. The Yamahas of Brian Reid, Jason Griffiths and Chris Fargher completed the top six. The only leaderboard change on lap two was that Lougher took third place from Reid. As the lap three times were posted Phillip was 11 seconds up on Joey

and Lougher, Reid and Griffiths retained their places but Ian Simpson (Honda) took sixth place from Fargher.

But on a dramatic last lap, Phillip McCallen ran out of fuel at Brandywell and Joey took victory number 17 from Brian Reid with Jason Griffiths in third place. Ian Simpson took fourth, Ian Lougher fifth and Gavin Lee (Yamaha) finished sixth, Chris Fargher having slid off at Governors Bridge on the last lap. Dunlop, Simpson and Lougher won the Manufacturers award.

Riding under the number that has become synonymous with Joey Dunlop, Ian Lougher exits Parliament Square, Ramsey.

The Castrol Honda team work on Hislop's RC45 prior to the start of the Senior

1994 Senior T.T. (six laps - 226.38 miles)

Steve Hislop   750 Honda   119.25 mph

On the Honda RC45, Steve Hislop completed a 750cc double with a start to finish victory.

He led Phillip McCallen after lap one by 19.4 seconds with Joey Dunlop third, 4.6 seconds down. Steve Ward (Honda), Jason Griffiths (Kawasaki) and Nigel Davies (Honda) made up the top six. The first three remained the same at the first pit stops, but with Steve Ward's retirement at Ramsey Hairpin, Griffiths moved up to fourth, Davies was fifth and Johnny Rea (Yamaha) took sixth place.

At half-distance Steve's lead was over one minute, and the only change to the leaderboard was that Davies took fourth place from Griffiths. There were no changes to the leaderboard after four laps, but two local riders, Gary Radcliffe

(Honda) and Paul Hunt (Yamaha) were chasing hard for a top six place.

The next leaderboard man to hit trouble was Johnny Rea who retired at the pits, so lap five saw Steve, Phillip and Joey out in front, followed by Nigel Davies, Jason Griffiths and Gary Radcliffe. Phillip McCallen set the fastest sixth lap of the race at 120.01 mph, but Steve took a comfortable 11th win by one minute 15 seconds with Joey giving Castrol Honda a 1-2-3.

Nigel Davies finished fourth ahead of Jason Griffiths and Gary Radcliffe. Sandra Barnett on her 750 Honda almost lapped at 110 mph, she recorded 109.98 mph, but retired at Sulby on the last lap.

Phillip McCallen once again set the fastest lap of the race, but had to give best to Steve Hislop. A Parliament Square shot.

Nigel Davies added to his T.T. tally with a fine fifth place; he is pictured just cranking into Quarter Bridge.

Still behind the bubble - Phillip leaps Ballaugh Bridge

1995 Formula 1 (six laps - 226.38 miles)

Phillip McCallen   750 Honda   117.84 mph

Phillip McCallen on the RC45 topped the practice leaderboard, but there was a strong Ducati challenge this year from Robert Holden, Iain Duffus and Simon Beck.

It was McCallen, with a lap at 120.85 mph, the fastest of the race, in front at the end of the first lap by 3.9 seconds from team-mate Joey Dunlop with Robert Holden in third place 11.9 seconds down. Simon Beck was fourth, followed by the Honda of Nick Jefferies and the Kawasaki of Jason Griffiths - Iain Duffus had retired at Ramsey. Lap two saw Joey the fastest and he led Phillip by 0.7 seconds at the first pit stops with the Ducatis of Beck and Holden next ahead of Jefferies and Griffiths.

The Honda duo swapped places again at half distance - Phillip had an advantage of 23.3 seconds, Beck was still third, Jefferies moved up to fourth and Colin Gable and Steve Ward brought their Hondas into the top six, Robert Holden having retired at the pits, and Jason Griffiths at Milntown after clipping the hedge there.

There were no changes to the top six on lap four, and Phillip was 35.4 seconds ahead. On lap five Joey was 27 seconds faster than Phillip and closed to within 8.2 seconds and the only leaderboard change was that Ward moved up to fifth with Chris Day (Kawasaki) taking sixth spot, Colin Gable having retired at the pits.

Phillip took the win from Joey by 18.1 seconds followed by Beck, Jefferies, Ward and Steve Linsdell (Yamaha), Chris Day had problems on the last lap and slowed to take 24th place.

Sandra Barnett on the Honda RC30 lapped at 111.57 mph, the fastest lady ever, to take 23rd place.

McCallen, Dunlop and Jefferies gave Honda the Manufacturers award.

Whilst the mechanics refuel and change the rear tyre on Steve Ward's machine, scrutineers check the safety of the machine.

Bradford's Nick Jefferies aviates at Ballacrye.

A dramatic last lap gave Mark Baldwin, seen here at Ballacraine, his debut T.T. win

1995 Ultra Lightweight T.T. (four laps - 150.92 miles)

Mark Baldwin   125 Honda   107.14 mph

A dramatic start to the 125cc race when Joey Dunlop, winner for the past three years, retired at the Hawthorn on the opening lap.

That really opened things up and at the end of the first lap Mick Lofthouse (Yamaha) led James Courtney (Honda) by 8.6 seconds with Mark Baldwin (Honda) in third place just half a second down on Courtney. The Hondas of Denis McCullough and Glen English and the Yamaha of Shaun Harris completed the top six.

Lofthouse led Courtney by five seconds at half distance, but Baldwin was just 0.1 seconds down in third, and the only leaderboard change saw Noel Clegg (Honda) taking fifth place with Glen English dropping to seventh. The only change in the top six after lap three was that English took over fifth spot, Clegg was sixth, Harris having retired at Creg-ny-Baa.

So into the final lap - Lofthouse led Courtney by 5.6 seconds with Baldwin 0.8 seconds down in third place. Mick Lofthouse finished first on the roads and looked a certain winner, but Mark Baldwin really flew around the final 37 miles, he shattered the lap record at 109.01 mph to snatch victory by 0.6 seconds with Courtney third followed by McCullough, Clegg and English.

Baldwin, Courtney and McCullough gave Honda the Manufacturers award.

James Courtney gasses the Irish Racing Motorcycles RS125 out of the Gooseneck.

Turn right at Ballacraine: Denis McCullough prepares for a quick run through the Glen Helen section.

Ready for the off - Joey is always calm at the start

1995 Lightweight T.T. (four laps - 150.92 miles)

Joey Dunlop   **250 Honda**   **115.68 mph** (record)

Joey Dunlop made no mistake in this race - he led James Courtney (Honda) by 13.8 seconds at the end of the first lap with Mick Lofthouse (Yamaha) tucked in behind the two Hondas.

Then came Phillip McCallen (Honda), Gavin Lee (Yamaha) and Mark Baldwin (Honda). The top three held station on lap two, Joey set the fastest lap of the race on lap two at 117.57 mph, Lee took fourth place from McCallen and Shaun Harris (Honda) took sixth place, with Baldwin slipping to ninth.

Joey led Courtney by 25.1 seconds at the end of lap three, Lee was up to third followed by McCallen, Harris and Lee Pullan (Yamaha), Mick Lofthouse had exhaust problems and dropped to 19th.

So it was win number 18 for Joey by 25.5 seconds from James Courtney with Gavin Lee in third place, 26 seconds down on Courtney. Phillip McCallen took fourth, Shaun Harris fifth and Denis McCullough sixth with Lee Pullan dropping to eighth

place. Mick Lofthouse cured his problems and finished in 13th place.

Dunlop, Courtney and McCallen won the Manufacturers award again for Honda.

A duo of Irish road-racing talent that must surely be vying for T.T. honours soon; Denis McCullough leads Gary Dynes into Ginger Hall on their RS 250 models.

A first T.T. win for Iain Duffus - with records for good measure

1995 Junior T.T. (four laps - 150.92 miles)

Iain Duffus   600 Honda   116.58 mph   (record)

The capacity for the Junior T.T. was raised to 600cc this year, replacing the Supersport 600 class, and Honda were all out for a clean sweep.

At the end of lap one they held the top six places - Iain Duffus led Phillip McCallen by 14.4 seconds with Bob Jackson 1.8 seconds down in third place. Colin Gable, Joey Dunlop and Nick Jefferies completed the leaderboard. Duffus had a 20-second advantage over McCallen after lap two - up to third place was Jefferies, Dunlop was fourth, Gable fifth and Steve Ward (Honda) took over sixth place with Bob Jackson down to eighth.

Lap three saw Duffus with a 13.1-second lead over McCallen with the only top six change seeing Gable taking

fourth place from Dunlop. Phillip McCallen really went for it on the final lap but found a neutral gear on the approach to the Waterworks Corners and slid off.

Iain Duffus took the chequered flag with a new lap record on his final lap at 117.87 mph and had just over a minute in hand over second place man Nick Jefferies. Colin Gable, Joey Dunlop and Steve Ward were next and Dave Leach brought his Yamaha into sixth place.

The first three riders won the Manufacturers award for Honda.

Nick Jefferies dwarfs his 600 Honda at Braddan Bridge

Colin Gable speeds through pit lane on his CBR600-based racer. On this standard-looking machine, he gained his first leaderboard place and helped Honda to win yet another team prize

The master at work - the inimitable style of Joey at Windy Corner

1995 Senior T.T. (six laps - 226.38 miles)

Joey Dunlop   750 Honda   119.11 mph

Those who thought that Joey's days of winning a 750cc T.T. race were over were in for a surprise in the Senior T.T.

A trio of Ducatis tried to wrest the Senior Trophy from Honda - but Joey held them off. Lap one saw him in front by 1.4 seconds from Iain Duffus with Simon Beck third, 1.9 seconds down and fourth place was held by Robert Holden - three Ducatis chasing Joey. The Hondas of Nick Jefferies and Steve Ward completed the top six. There were no changes to the leaderboard after lap two had been completed, and Joey had stretched his lead to 3.7 seconds - eight seconds covered the first three.

Joey led at half-distance by 18.6 seconds from Duffus, Jefferies moved up to third, Beck was fourth, Ward fifth and David Goodley (Kawasaki) took sixth place - Robert Holden had parted company with his Ducati on the exit from Governors Bridge. The order after lap four read - Dunlop, Duffus, Jefferies, Ward, Goodley and Beck. The top five remained the same after lap five had been completed but Chris Day (Kawasaki) took sixth spot with Beck slowing to eighth.

Joey notched up win number 19 by 33.5 seconds from Iain Duffus, and with the fastest lap of the race on lap six at 121.73 mph, Steve Ward snatched third place from Nick Jefferies by 2.7 seconds. David Goodley finished fifth and Bob Jackson (Kawasaki) took sixth place from Chris Day who finished seventh.

Joey, Steve and Nick took the Manufacturers award.

Nick Jefferies has excelled in all forms of motorcycle sport, a great ambassador for Honda, pictured at Braddan Bridge.

Win number one for Phillip McCallen in 1996

1996 T.T. Formula 1 (six laps - 226.38 miles)

Phillip McCallen   750 Honda   116.18 mph

Phillip McCallen was the firm favourite for F1 honours, and sure enough at the end of the first lap he was in the lead by 6.9 seconds from Honda-mounted Iain Duffus with Nick Jefferies in third place on his Honda a further 14.2 seconds down. Lee Pullan (Yamaha), Michael Rutter (Ducati) and Jim Moodie (Kawasaki) completed the leaderboard.

There were no changes after lap two had been completed and Phillip's advantage was up to 21.6 seconds - Jason Griffiths (Honda) was on a charge, 10th at the end of the first lap, a quick circuit moved him up to seventh.

The pit stops had made quite a difference to the third lap times - Phillip still led but from Lee Pullan by 42.4 seconds. Nick Jefferies was third, Michael Rutter fourth, Jason Griffiths fifth and Jim Moodie sixth - Iain Duffus had dropped to ninth.

At the second round of pit stops the top five remained the same, but Iain Duffus was back up to sixth with Jim Moodie dropping to 16th. Lee Pullan's great challenge ended at the pits, he had problems getting a new rear tyre, he eventually got away but dropped at the end of lap five to 14th. At the end of lap five Phillip led Nick Jefferies by 52.3 seconds followed by Rutter, Duffus - who set the fastest lap of the race at 120.84 mph - Griffiths and new sixth place man Jim Hodson (750 Kawasaki). The top five remained the same to the flag, and sixth place was taken by Marc Flynn (Kawasaki) with Jim Hodson finishing eighth - Lee Pullan retired at the Creg on the last lap.

McCallen, Jefferies and Duffus won the Manufacturers award.

A pensive Joey waits for his mechanics to change wheels on the awesome RC45 before the start of the Formula One race.

Local hero Mike Casey points the Martin Bullock-entered RC30 skyward off Sulby Bridge. Mike won the 1995 Senior Manx Grand Prix on this machine, which had already won the 1994 Manx with Brian Venables aboard.

Another Lightweight win for the incredible Dunlop

1996 Lightweight T.T. (three laps - 113.19 miles)

Joey Dunlop   250 Honda   115.31 mph

Phillip McCallen, who had come so close to winning this race in previous years, set off in determined mood. After the first lap he was in the lead, but by just 0.2 seconds from Joey Dunlop, with Jim Moodie making it a Honda 1-2-3 by holding third place, 5.3 seconds down.

Then came Denis McCullough (Honda), Jason Griffiths (Honda) and Ian Lougher (Yamaha). McCallen increased his lead over Dunlop to 2.1 seconds with the fastest lap of the race at 116.94 mph, with Moodie a further 10 seconds down, and the only leaderboard change was that Nigel Davies (Yamaha) took sixth place from Lougher. But then McCallen began to suffer from exhaust problems and slowed - Joey took

advantage and at the end of lap three took over in front by 10.9 seconds, but from Moodie with McCallen in third place. Griffiths, Davies and McCullough made up the leaderboard.

Joey notched up another win by 5.7 seconds from Jim Moodie with Jason Griffiths taking third place from a slowing Phillip McCallen. Nigel Davies and Denis McCullough completed the top six.

The first three in the race gave the Manufacturers award to Honda.

Thirty-seven and a half miles gone, and still together; Jason Griffiths (2) leads Nigel Davies through Governors Bridge near the end of lap one.

Joey Dunlop, pictured with Davy Wood. The pairing have made the T.T. success, Joey with his riding skill and Davy in charge of the pits and refuelling. Davy also grooms the up-and-coming Irish riders, preparing them for the Manx Grand Prix and, ultimately, the T.T.

A fourth 125 T.T. win for Joey Dunlop

1996 Ultra Lightweight T.T. (two laps - 75.46 miles)

Joey Dunlop **125 Honda** **106.33 mph**

Because of poor weather conditions this race was reduced in distance from four laps to two, making it a real sprint and no pit stops necessary.

Joey Dunlop was all out to regain the 125cc title he had lost in 1995, but at the end of the opening lap it was Gavin Lee on his Honda who led Joey by 1.5 seconds. Third place was held by Glen English (Honda), Ian Lougher (JWS) was fourth, Bob Heath (Honda) fifth and Gary Dynes (Honda) completed the leaderboard.

Could Joey, with his greater experience, peg Gavin Lee back? At Glen Helen on the final lap Lee still led by two seconds. By the time they reached Ramsey Hairpin Joey was in front, but by just 0.2 seconds - the Mountain would decide.

Joey flashed over the final miles with a lap at 107.62 mph to take victory number 21 by 3.8 seconds from Gavin Lee. The rest of the leaderboard remained unchanged, and of the 31 finishers, 29 rode the 125cc single-cylinder, two-stroke Honda.

Dunlop, Lee and English took the Manufacturers award.

Gavin Lee, pictured here at Waterworks, made Joey Dunlop work hard for his 21st victory.

Model maker and model racer, Cornwall's finest current road-racer Glen English steadies the plot for Signpost Corner.

Phillip's second win of the week

1996 Junior T.T. (three laps - 113.19 miles)

Phillip McCallen   600 Honda   117.65 mph

The Junior race was reduced from four laps to three because of weather problems, but it didn't stop Phillip McCallen smashing the lap and race records!

He opened with a new lap record at 118.94 mph to lead Iain Duffus (Honda) by 14.5 seconds with the Honda of Ian Simpson in third place, 15 seconds back. Nigel Davies had his Kawasaki in fourth place ahead of the Hondas of Jim Moodie and Colin Gable.

Lap two saw McCallen in the lead by 35.8 seconds, but from Simpson who was 12.2 seconds up on Duffus who had pitted at the end of the first lap. Moodie was fourth, Jason Griffiths (Honda) and Nick Jefferies (Honda) came on to the leaderboard with Davies and Gable sixth and seventh.

Phillip won his second race of the week by 17.9 seconds

from Iain Duffus with Ian Simpson completing a Honda top three. The rest of the leaderboard read - Colin Gable, Jason Griffiths and Nigel Davies.

The first three finishers gave Honda another Manufacturers award.

Phillip McCallen adds another win to his T.T. tally.

Currently the fastest-lapping female on the T.T. course, Sandra Barnett takes Sulby Bridge in fine style.

Phillip on his way to a first T.T. hat-trick

1996 Production Race (three laps - 113.19 miles)

Phillip McCallen   900 Honda   117.32 mph (record)

The Production race was re-introduced to the programme for 1996 and held over three laps of the course on the Friday morning.

The 900 Hondas of Iain Duffus and Phillip McCallen started a race-long battle on the opening lap and Duffus held the advantage by 3.6 seconds with Nigel Davies (Yamaha) in third place, 3.6 seconds adrift. Then came Colin Gable (Honda) and the Yamahas of Tim Leech and Lee Pullan.

Both McCallen and Duffus lapped at over 118 mph second time around, but Phillip was the faster at 118.93 mph and took the lead by 3.1 seconds followed by Pullan, Davies, Alan

Bennallick (Honda) and Nick Jefferies (Honda). Tim Leech retired at the pits and Colin Gable dropped to ninth.

So it was win number three of the week for McCallen, by 6.1 seconds from Duffus with Davies in third place. Colin Gable, Lee Pullan and Derek Young (Honda) completed the top six - Nick Jefferies finished seventh just ahead of Alan Bennallick.

Honda took the Ultimate Test Ride award.

Gooseneck action; Iain Duffus and the V & M CBR900RR, a close pursuer to the all-conquering McCallen.

Heading for a text-book landing, Colin Gable sets the Carbontek CBR900RR on course at Ballaugh Bridge.

Joey • Phillip • Nick
Another Honda 1 - 2 - 3
And McCallen becomes the first rider to win four T.T. races in a week

1996 Senior T.T. (six laps - 226.38 miles)

Phillip McCallen   750 Honda   119.76 mph

In 1961 Mike Hailwood came close to winning four races in a week until he retired in the Junior with just 14 miles to go with a comfortable lead.

Could the Portadown Flyer become the first rider in the history of the races to achieve this feat? He opened with a lap at 121.69 mph to lead Jim Moodie (Kawasaki) by 7.2 seconds with the Honda of Nick Jefferies in third place 12.5 seconds down. Bob Jackson had his Kawasaki in fourth place, Michael Rutter's Ducati was fifth followed by Jason Griffiths (Honda). Phillip increased his lead to 13.5 seconds after two laps with the fastest lap of the race at 122.14 mph, and the only top six change was that Lee Pullan (Yamaha) took sixth place from Griffiths.

No changes in the top three at half-distance, but Joey Dunlop (Honda) jumped up to fourth ahead of Jackson and Pullan. Lap four and McCallen's lead was over one minute from Moodie with Jefferies, Dunlop, Jackson and Pullan chasing. Jim Moodie's brave effort ended in retirement at the pits so lap five saw McCallen with a lead of 70 seconds from Jefferies while Joey was up to third followed by Jackson, Pullan

and Derek Young (Honda) - Griffiths was seventh just ahead of Rutter.

History was made as Phillip McCallen crossed the line to win his fourth race of the week at 119.76 mph and by one minute 12.4 seconds - but Joey Dunlop set the fastest sixth lap of the race at 121.89 mph to snatch second place from Nick Jefferies by just 1.9 seconds. Bob Jackson, Lee Pullan and Derek Young made up the final leaderboard of the week. Michael Rutter retired at the pits and Jason Griffiths took seventh place. Again the first three finishers took the Manufacturers award for Honda.

A classic shot that typifies T.T. racing. With the drop down from Kate's Cottage behind him, Joey Dunlop makes light work of Creg ny Baa.

Phillip McCallen winds open the throttle, dumps the clutch and prepares to ride off into the distance for his fourth win of the week.

On his way to his third successive Formula One win - Phillip McCallen

1997 T.T. Formula 1 (six laps - 226.38 miles)

Phillip McCallen   750 Honda   119.90 mph

Phillip McCallen, winner of this race for the past two years, was the firm favourite to collect a hat-trick of wins.

Sure enough, at the end of the opening circuit, with the fastest lap of the race at 122.98 mph, he was in front by 4.3 seconds from team-mate Joey Dunlop with Michael Rutter on the RVF750 in third place, 8.4 seconds down. Then came Simon Beck (Kawasaki), Ian Simpson (Honda) and Marc Flynn (Honda). Phillip extended his lead to 11.3 seconds at the end of lap two, and the only leaderboard change was that Flynn took fifth place from Simpson.

Half distance saw the gap between the leaders up to 16.6 seconds, but it was Michael Rutter in second place with Simon Beck third, Marc Flynn was fourth, Joey had slipped to fifth and Bob Jackson (Kawasaki) took sixth place with Ian Simpson down to seventh.

There were more changes on lap four - the two leaders remained the same but Flynn moved up to third, Jackson was fourth, Joey still fifth and Simpson back up to sixth. Simon Beck had a lap some four minutes slower than the leaders and dropped to 13th. Whilst McCallen and Rutter continued at the front - lap five saw Jackson third, Simpson fourth, Dunlop fifth and Flynn sixth.

So Phillip McCallen completed his hat-trick of wins by 35.7 seconds from Michael Rutter with Bob Jackson in third place. Ian Simpson, Marc Flynn and Joey Dunlop completed the leaderboard.

McCallen, Rutter and Simpson took the Manufacturers award.

The two sides of V & M Honda Britain team; left, Michael Rutter is captured at Tower Bends and right, Ian Simpson skirts the farmyard wall at Ballacraine.

Win number 22 coming up for Joey Dunlop

1997 Lightweight T.T. (four laps - 150.92 miles)

Joey Dunlop   250 Honda   115.59 mph

Joey Dunlop notched up T.T. victory number 22, but for the first two laps he had a terrific scrap with Phillip McCallen.

When the first lap times were posted Dunlop led by 1.2 seconds, with Ian Lougher (Honda) in third place 7.9 seconds down. Gary Dynes (Honda) was fourth ahead of John McGuinness (Aprilia) and and Shaun Harris (Yamaha). Joey and Phillip lapped at identical speeds on lap two - 116.71 mph - so the 1.2 seconds difference remained, and Dynes took over third place from Lougher. Joey had a much better pit stop than Phillip, and the times from Glen Helen showed that he was 18 seconds in front. But then at Quarry Bends Phillip came off in a big way, he escaped with just cuts and bruises, but Joey was well away now.

At the end of lap three he had a lead of almost one minute from Dynes, Lougher was third, Harris fourth, McGuinness fifth and the new sixth place man was Derek Young (Honda).

Joey took the chequered flag by 47 seconds, but from Ian Lougher - John McGuinness with the fastest lap of the race at 116.83 mph took third spot. Shaun Harris took fourth place, and Gary Dynes, with the slowest last lap of the top six finished fifth ahead of Derek Young.

Dunlop, Lougher and Dynes took the Manufacturers award.

A good viewing spot - with good refreshments on hand - Marc Flynn rounds the corner named after the pub, or was it the other way round?

Derek Young rounds Governors Bridge.

It was lap and race records for Ian Lougher

1997 Ultra Lightweight T.T. (four laps - 150.92 miles)

Ian Lougher   **125 Honda**   **107.89 mph** (record)

At the end of the opening lap the first 16 riders were all on Hondas, and out in front with a lap at 108.60 mph, and 2.1 seconds in front was Denis McCullough.

Second place was held by Ian Lougher with Glen English in third spot. Robert Dunlop, making his comeback after his Ballaugh Bridge crash three years before, held a fine fourth place ahead of big brother Joey and Gavin Lee.

No change at the top at half-distance, McCullough stretched his lead to 7.2 seconds, but Owen McNally was in fifth place with Joey down to eighth. With one lap to go McCullough led Lougher by just half a second!! What a last lap to look forward to. Robert Dunlop took third place from English and Lee moved ahead of McNally. The two leaders sped around the course on the final lap - at Glen Helen they couldn't be separated on time - at Ramsey Hairpin McCullough led by two seconds - Lougher turned up the power on the Mountain section and with a new lap record at 109.25 mph, snatched victory by 2.1 seconds with Robert Dunlop a popular third. English, McNally and Lee completed the top six, and Joey took a bronze replica for 10th place.

The first three took the Manufacturers award.

Rodeo style for runner-up Denis McCullough at Ballaugh Bridge.

Seven years after his only other T.T. win, Ian Lougher is interviewed by Radio T.T.'s Geoff Cannell.

Ian Simpson's first T.T. win was at record speed on the V & M CBR600

1997 Junior T.T. (four laps - 150.92 miles)

Ian Simpson **600 Honda** **118.41 mph** (record)

Just 48 hours after his high speed get off, Phillip McCallen was on the starting line for the four-lap Junior T.T., but at the end of the first lap it was the Honda of Ian Simpson who led McCallen by 9.8 seconds with Derek Young in third place. Michael Rutter, Bob Jackson and Jason Griffiths, all on Hondas completed the leaderboard.

With a new lap record on lap two at 119.86 mph, Simpson increased his lead over McCallen 23.2 seconds with Young still third, Rutter fourth, Jackson fifth but with Jason Griffiths retirement at Hillberry, Joey Dunlop moved into sixth place. Lap three saw the rampant Simpson's lead extended to just under 30 seconds and the only change to the top six was that Rutter took third place from Young by 2.3 seconds.

Ian Simpson scored his first T.T. win in record-breaking style from Phillip McCallen and Michael Rutter. Derek Young held fourth place, but Joey Dunlop pipped Bob Jackson for fifth place by nine seconds.

With the first seven riders on Hondas it was no surprise that they took the Manufacturers award through the first three.

Michael Rutter gets his 600 Honda airborne at Ballacrye.

More records for the battered and bruised 'Portadown Flyer'

1997 Production Race (two laps - 75.46 miles)

Phillip McCallen   900 Honda   117.12 mph

Weather conditions resulted in the Production Race being reduced from three laps to two, and the battle between the Honda of Phillip McCallen and the Ducati of Ian Simpson was eagerly awaited by the fans.

After one lap Phillip had the advantage over Ian by 11.5 seconds with Simon Beck's Honda in third place - 13.7 seconds down. Marc Flynn (750 Suzuki) was fourth followed by the Hondas of Alan Bennallick and Derek Young. Jim Hodson was seventh on his Yamaha, and all top seven had lapped in under 20 minutes.

Phillip McCallen took his second Production race victory and his second win of the week by 7.6 seconds from Ian Simpson and the only change to the top six was that Jim Hodson took fifth place with Alan Bennallick dropping to seventh spot.

McCallen, Beck and Young took the Manufacturers award. The Honda CBR900RR Fireblade took the Ultimate Test Ride award.

Sponsored by Motorcycle Sport and Leisure magazine, Allan Bennallick swings his Fireblade through Braddan Bridge.

Three wins this week for works Honda rider Phillip McCallen - and 11 in all

1997 Senior T.T. (six laps - 226.38 miles)

Phillip McCallen   750 Honda   119.55 mph

Phillip McCallen was all out to complete another hat-trick of wins in the final race of the week. For the first time ever the starting order for the Senior was decided on the overall practice leaderboard, so McCallen was No. 1 with Joey Dunlop at an unfamiliar No. 5.

At the end of lap one Phillip was in front of the NSR500 Honda V-twin of Jim Moodie by 5.4 seconds with Simon Beck's Kawasaki in third place, 11.5 seconds down. The Hondas of Ian Simpson, Marc Flynn and Derek Young made up the first lap leaderboard.

Just 10.8 seconds was the difference after lap two and the only change to the top six was that Bob Jackson took his Kawasaki into sixth place with Young in seventh. Jim Moodie closed in on Phillip McCallen after three laps - the difference was nine seconds. Bob Jackson, who had gone for three laps on a tank of fuel was up to third followed by Simpson,

Beck and Flynn.

After four laps had been completed the order was McCallen by 18.3 seconds from Moodie, Simpson, Beck, Flynn and Joey Dunlop with Jackson in seventh place. Lap five and the top three remained the same, but Jackson was now fourth, followed by Beck and Young with Joey seventh. The race pattern didn't alter on the final lap and with the fastest lap of the race at 122.22 mph, Phillip McCallen brought his total of wins at the T.T. to 11. The first three took the Manufacturers award.

Jim Moodie swings the Grand-Prix spec NSR500 V-twin through Parliament Square, trying, without success, to catch Phillip McCallen.

Phillip McCallen reflects on another 'good week in the office', a further three T.T. wins to his name.

Honda Milestones of the 120 mph era

1st Honda 120+ lap	Steve Hislop	120.92 mph	Formula One	1989
25th Honda 120+ lap	Steve Hislop	122.94 mph	Senior	1991
50th Honda 120+ lap	Steve Hislop	120.47 mph	Formula One	1994
75th Honda 120+ lap	Joey Dunlop	120.14 mph	Senior	1996
100th Honda 120+ lap	Ian Simpson	120.84 mph	Senior	1997

Totals per Manufacturer

	1989	1990	1991	1992	1993	1994	1995	1996	1997	
Honda	**8**	**4**	**17**	**10**	**6**	**13**	**10**	**9**	**24**	**101**
Yamaha	-	-	5	9	-	-	-	1	-	15
Norton	-	-	1	12	-	-	-	-	-	13
Ducati	-	-	-	-	1	-	7	-	-	8
Kawasaki	-	-	-	-	-	-	-	3	5	8

Riders who have achieved 120+ mph laps on Honda

Phillip McCallen	31	Michael Rutter	3
Steve Hislop	23	Ian Simpson	3
Joey Dunlop	17	Steve Ward	2
Nick Jefferies	8	Brian Morrison	2
Carl Fogarty	5	Iain Duffus	1
Jim Moodie	4	Derek Young	1
Marc Flynn	3		

Index of Honda T.T. finishers 1959 - 1997

Adrien, Patrick
- 1997 Production — 56

Ahearn, Jack
- 1975 Production 10 lap — 24

Aldrick, Malcolm
- 1974 S/car 500 — 7
- 1975 S/car 1000 — 11

Alflatt, Brian
- 1995 S/car A — 25
- 1995 S/car B — 42
- 1996 S/car A — 27
- 1996 S/car B — 24

Allen, Mick
- 1966 50cc — 9
- 1967 Lightweight 125 — 29

Anderson, Tony
- 1992 Lightweight 125 — 26
- 1993 Lightweight 125 — 13
- 1994 Lightweight 125 — 12
- 1996 Lightweight 125 — =19
- 1997 Lightweight — 34
- 1997 Lightweight 125 — 26

Archibald, Adrian
- 1997 Formula 1 — 13
- 1997 Junior — 7
- 1997 Production — 13
- 1997 Senior — 11

Arian, Richard
- 1977 Formula 2 — 8

Armer, Joss
- 1996 Lightweight — 39
- 1996 Lightweight 125 — 29
- 1997 Lightweight — 18

Armes, Phil
- 1985 Production 250 — 14
- 1987 Formula 2 — 19
- 1988 Production C — 23
- 1989 SS600 — 16
- 1992 Lightweight 125 — 16

Armstrong, Ian
- 1996 Junior — 34

Armstrong, Ken
- 1970 Lightweight 125 — 10

Ashcroft, Raymond
- 1972 Production 500 — 10

Ashford, Kevin
- 1996 Lightweight — 36

Ashton, Dave
- 1988 Production C — 40
- 1989 SS600 — 18

Ashton, George
- 1965 50cc — 9

Ayers, Alex
- 1975 Production 10 lap — 28

Ayles, Martin
- 1991 Junior — 20

Baker, John
- 1993 Lightweight 125 — 20

Baldock, Geoffrey
- 1991 SS400 — 14
- 1991 SS600 — 12

Baldwin, Mark
- 1995 Lightweight 125 — 1
- 1995 Lightweight — 10

Barker, Bill
- 1969 Lightweight 125 — 14
- 1970 Lightweight 125 — 16
- 1971 Lightweight 125 — 14
- 1971 Production 250 — 9
- 1972 Lightweight 125 — 15
- 1973 Lightweight 125 — 19
- 1974 Lightweight 125 — 22
- 1978 Formula 3 — 10

Barker, Ross
- 1993 Lightweight 125 — 19
- 1995 Lightweight 125 — 23

Barnett, Sandra
- 1994 Formula 1 — 33
- 1994 SS600 — 39
- 1994 SS400 — 15
- 1995 Formula 1 — 23
- 1995 Junior — 28
- 1995 Senior — 31
- 1996 Formula 1 — 20
- 1996 Junior — 12
- 1996 Production — 27
- 1997 Junior — 15
- 1997 Production — 25

Barrett, Paul
- 1983 Formula 2 — 23

Barton, Chris
- 1989 Lightweight 125 — 13
- 1993 Lightweight 125 — 18

Barton, David
- 1968 Lightweight 125 — 20
- 1969 Lightweight 125 — 11
- 1974 Lightweight 125 — 19

Barton, John
- 1991 Lightweight 125 — 16
- 1992 Formula 1 — 20
- 1992 Senior — 12
- 1994 Formula 1 — 11
- 1996 Junior — 20
- 1996 Production — 28

Barton, Nigel
- 1988 Production B — 28
- 1990 Formula 1 — 11
- 1990 SS600 — 20
- 1990 Senior — 10

Bastiansen, Torbjorn
- 1988 Formula 1 — 33
- 1989 Production 750 — 22

Bates, Derrick
- 1984 Production A — 11
- 1988 Production C — 53
- 1989 Senior — 24

Bates, Michael
- 1994 S/car A — 42
- 1994 S/car B — 26

Bateson, Peter
- 1985 Production 250 — 7
- 1986 Production D — 4
- 1987 Formula 2 — 11
- 1987 Production D — 10

Batson, Alan
- 1987 Formula 2 — 15
- 1988 Production C — 6
- 1992 SS600 — 12
- 1993 SS600 — 9
- 1995 Junior — 12
- 1996 Junior — 18
- 1996 Production — 16

Baylie, Ron
- 1972 Production 750 — 10

Beale, Bruce
- 1964 Lightweight 125 — 6
- 1964 Junior — 11
- 1965 Junior — 4

Beaud, Y.
- 1984 Formula 1 — 21

Beck, Simon
- 1992 Formula 1 — 13
- 1993 Formula 1 — 7
- 1993 SS600 — 3
- 1994 SS600 — 16
- 1995 Junior — 14
- 1997 Junior — 9
- 1997 Production — 3

Bell, Douglas
- 1997 Formula 1 — 32
- 1997 Production — 50

Bennallick, Alan
- 1993 Formula 1 — 11
- 1993 Senior — 7
- 1994 Formula 1 — 19
- 1994 SS600 — 17
- 1994 Senior — 12
- 1996 Formula 1 — 12
- 1996 Production — 8
- 1996 Senior — 12
- 1997 Formula 1 — 7
- 1997 Production — 7
- 1997 Senior — 9

Bennett, Garry
- 1993 Lightweight 125 — 5
- 1995 Lightweight 125 — 8
- 1996 Lightweight 125 — 9
- 1997 Lightweight 125 — 13

Bentman, Graham
- 1977 Formula 3 — 4
- 1979 Formula 1 — 21
- 1979 Formula 2 — 31
- 1979 Schweppes Cl. — 31
- 1981 Formula 2 — 8

Bevan, Colin
- 1986 Production D — 13
- 1987 Formula 2 — 20
- 1987 Production D — 17

Bexley, Dave
- 1973 S/car 500 — 19
- 1974 S/car 750 — 8

Bhathena, Aspi
- 1987 Production D — 37

Biggs, Geoff
- 1973 Production 250 — 15

Birkinshaw, Martin
- 1988 Production C — 30

Bisbey, Roy
- 1975 Production 10 lap — 42

Black, David
- 1996 Production — 33

Blengl, Manfred
- 1992 SS600 — 23

Boast, Pete
- 1988 Production C — 24
- 1988 Junior — 16
- 1993 SS600 — 15
- 1993 Senior — 28

Boddice, Mick Jnr
- 1994 S/car A — 17
- 1994 S/car B — 13
- 1995 S/car B — 11
- 1997 S/car A — 12
- 1997 S/car B — 26

Boddice, Mick
- 1990 S/car A — 2
- 1990 S/car B — 23
- 1991 S/car A — 1
- 1991 S/car B — 1
- 1992 S/car A — 3
- 1992 S/car B — 2
- 1994 S/car A — 3
- 1994 S/car B — 3
- 1995 S/car A — 2
- 1995 S/car B — 3
- 1996 S/car A — 5
- 1997 S/car B — 8

Boldman, Bill
- 1994 SS600 — 63
- 1996 Lightweight — 48
- 1996 Junior — =51
- 1997 Lightweight — 33
- 1997 Junior — 40

Bonhui, Bruno
- 1997 Junior — 44

Booth, John
- 1992 S/car A — 13
- 1992 S/car B — 15
- 1993 S/car A — 13

Year	Class	No.
1993	S/car B	12
1995	S/car A	30
1997	S/car A	29
1997	S/car B	31
Bosson, Lars		
1994	SS600	36
Boughey, Roy		
1967	Lightweight 125	12
1969	Lightweight 250	13
1972	Production 500	9
Bowie, David		
1991	Formula 1	20
Bowler, Roger		
1973	Formula 750	12
1977	Formula 1	11
1977	Jubilee	20
1979	Formula 1	6
1979	Formula 2	2
Boyd, Wade		
1993	SS600	32
1993	Senior	38
1994	Formula 1	34
1994	SS600	31
Boyes, Steve		
1986	Formula 2	32
1986	Production C	8
1986	Production D	11
1987	Formula 2	16
1989	Formula 1	27
1989	Production 750	16
Bradford, Bertie		
1990	Lightweight 125	33
1991	Lightweight 125	33
1993	Lightweight 125	24
1994	Lightweight 125	27
1995	Lightweight 125	29
Brady, Paschal		
1994	S/car A	44
1994	S/car B	37
1995	S/car A	45
1995	S/car B	43
Brandon, John		
1972	S/car 750	4
1973	S/car 750	3
1985	S/car A	42
Brennan, Gerry		
1985	Production 250	8
1991	SS400	36
Brew, Andy		
1987	Production D	29
Brewer, Rob		
1983	Formula 2	14
1984	Formula 2	19
Briscoe, Frank		
1994	S/car B	38
1995	S/car A	33
1995	S/car B	31
1997	S/car A	25
1997	S/car B	27
Brock, W.		
1963	Lightweight 250	18
Brown, Bob		
1960	Lightweight 250	4
Brown, Dave		
1994	Lightweight 125	11
1996	Lightweight 125	30
Brown, Shawn		
1995	Lightweight 125	26
1996	Lightweight 125	16
Brown, Wattie		
1994	Formula 1	18
1995	Formula 1	25
1995	Senior	20
1997	Junior	22
1997	Senior	33
Browning, Dave		
1967	Lightweight 125	17
Bryan, Nigel		
1991	SS600	30
Bryans, Ralph		
1963	Lightweight 125	9
1964	Lightweight 125	3
1964	50cc	2
1965	Lightweight 125	6
1966	Lightweight 125	7
1966	50cc	1
1967	Lightweight 250	3
Buckley, Keith		
1980	Formula 1	6
1983	Formula 1	16
1983	Senior Classic	24
Bull, Steve		
1985	Production 250	27
Burnett, Roger		
1985	Senior	8
1986	Senior	22
1986	Production C	6
1986	Production D	19
1986	Senior	1
1988	Production C	27
1988	Formula 1	3
1988	Senior	5
Butenuth, Hans Otto		
1969	Lightweight 250	17
1980	Formula 1	11
1980	Formula 2	6
1982	Formula 1	11
1983	Formula 2	13
1985	Formula 1	51
1985	Senior	37
1988	Production B	33
1989	SS600	36
1990	Formula 1	38
1990	Senior	27
1991	SS600	26
1992	SS600	30
1993	SS600	39
Byers, Eddie		
1987	Production B	40
Caffrey, John		
1979	Formula 3	15
1980	Formula 2	16
Cain, Michael		
1990	Lightweight 125	15
Cameron, Rob		
1996	S/car B	16
1997	S/car A	11
1997	S/car B	7
Campbell, Crichton		
1989	SS600	39
1991	SS400	20
Cannell, Graham		
1986	Junior	3
Carpenter, Phil		
1973	Production 250	6
Carruthers, Kel		
1966	Lightweight 125	12
1967	Lightweight 125	5
1967	Lightweight 125	3
Carswell, Gary		
1996	Production	25
1997	Production	14
Casement, Dennis		
1976	Production 10 lap	41
1977	Formula 2	3
1978	Formula 1	9
1978	Formula 2	9
Casey, Mike		
1988	Production C	38
1995	Formula 1	17
1996	Junior	26
Castle, David		
1992	SS600	18
1993	Formula 1	25
1993	SS600	19
1994	Formula 1	39
1994	SS600	52
1997	Junior	28
1997	Production	35
Caughey, Alan		
1990	Lightweight 125	4
1992	Lightweight 125	10
1993	Lightweight 125	7
1994	Lightweight	9
Chadwick, Alan		
1963	Lightweight 125	32
Chapman, John		
1965	Lightweight 125	18
1967	Lightweight 125	13
Chatterton, Mick		
1979	Formula 2	18
1989	Lightweight 125	19
1990	Lightweight 125	10
1991	Lightweight 125	24
1992	Lightweight 125	28
1993	Lightweight 125	16
1993	Junior	27
1994	Lightweight 125	14
1994	Junior	24
1995	Lightweight 125	18
1995	Lightweight	27
1996	Lightweight	25
1996	Lightweight 125	14
1997	Lightweight	29
1997	Lightweight 125	27
Cheung, Simon		
1989	Formula 1	42
Childs, John		
1995	S/car A	18
1995	S/car B	48
1996	S/car A	8
1996	S/car B	6
Christensen, Peter Marcussen		
1992	SS600	37
Claude, Rob		
1983	Formula 2	29
Clark, Martin		
1994	S/car B	14
Clay, Stuart		
1992	Lightweight 125	37
Clegg, Noel		
1991	Lightweight 125	8
1992	Lightweight 125	9
1994	Lightweight 125	4
1995	Lightweight 125	5
1996	Lightweight 125	7
1997	Lightweight 125	8
Clegg, Steve		
1996	Lightweight 125	31
Coates, Richard		
1986	Production D	14
1992	Lightweight 125	20
Cookson, Mike		
1995	S/car A	40
1995	S/car B	34
1996	S/car A	39
1997	S/car A	21
1997	S/car B	23
Copeland, Alistair		
1980	Formula 1	10
1982	Formula 1	13
Cornbill, Fred		
1973	S/car 500	16
1974	S/car 750	28
1974	S/car 500	12
1975	S/car 1000	13
1976	S/car 1000	20
Corner, Charlie		
1988	Production C	31
1989	Formula 1	11
Cornes, Eric		
1975	Production 10 lap	22
Courtney, James		
1994	Junior	7
1995	Lightweight 125	3
1995	Lightweight	2
1995	Junior	24
Coxon, Ron		
1972	S/car 750	28
Cranston, Paul		
1984	Formula 1	74
1988	Production C	33
1990	Formula 1	25
1991	Formula 1	18

Crellin, John

Year	Class	Pos
1990	SS600	30
1992	Formula 1	30
1992	Senior	22

Crew, Chris

Year	Class	Pos
1990	Senior	28

Crew, Peter

Year	Class	Pos
1974	Production 500	10

Crick, John

Year	Class	Pos
1977	Formula 1	29
1977	Formula 2	4
1977	Jubilee	36
1980	Formula 2	19

Cross, Anthony

Year	Class	Pos
1995	Junior	35
1995	Senior	36
1996	Formula 1	30
1996	Junior	35
1996	Senior	28
1997	Junior	23
1997	Senior	27

Crossley, Richard

Year	Class	Pos
1993	S/car A	6
1993	S/car B	3

Crowe, Cathal

Year	Class	Pos
1990	Lightweight 125	31

Crumpton, James

Year	Class	Pos
1995	Lightweight 125	11
1997	Lightweight 125	23

Cull, Steve

Year	Class	Pos
1982	Formula 1	15
1985	Junior	2
1986	Junior	1
1987	Formula 2	17
1988	Junior	6

Curry, Fred

Year	Class	Pos
1964	Lightweight 125	15
1965	Lightweight 125	14
1966	Lightweight 125	9
1966	Lightweight 250	14
1967	Lightweight 125	6
1970	Lightweight 125	6

Curry, Jim

Year	Class	Pos
1970	Lightweight 250	25
1973	Production 250	7
1973	Lightweight 125	21
1984	Classic Historic 350	9

Curtin, Mark

Year	Class	Pos
1990	Lightweight 125	28
1991	Lightweight 125	13

Cusick, Thomas

Year	Class	Pos
1996	Lightweight 125	28

Dahne, Helmut

Year	Class	Pos
1978	Formula 1	4
1979	Formula 1	8
1984	Premier Classic	24
1984	Production B	2
1994	Formula 1	15
1994	SS600	21

Danks. Dave

Year	Class	Pos
1975	Production 10 lap	25
1976	Production 10 lap	25

Darvill, Peter

Year	Class	Pos
1971	Production 750	10
1971	Formula 750	9
1975	Production 10 lap	44
1976	Production 10 lap	34

Davies, Nigel

Year	Class	Pos
1994	Formula 1	6
1994	SS600	12
1994	Senior	4
1995	Junior	7
1996	Formula 1	11
1996	Senior	9

Davies, Peter

Year	Class	Pos
1988	Production C	34
1988	Junior	29

Davis, Wendy

Year	Class	Pos
1997	S/car A	42
1997	S/car B	41

Dawson, Gary

Year	Class	Pos
1996	Lightweight 125	26
1997	Lightweight 125	30

Day, Chris

Year	Class	Pos
1993	Formula 1	13
1993	Senior	10
1994	SS600	11
1994	Senior	7
1995	Junior	20

Day, Paul

Year	Class	Pos
1994	Lightweight 125	17
1995	Lightweight 125	21

Dean, David

Year	Class	Pos
1984	Production B	3
1987	Formula 2	8
1988	Production C	18
1988	Senior	35

Dearden, Dave

Year	Class	Pos
1984	Formula 1	56
1985	Senior	36
1986	Production C	13

Degerholm, Blair

Year	Class	Pos
1995	Senior	29
1996	Lightweight	42
1996	Junior	36
1997	Formula 1	26
1997	Production	46

Dewar, John

Year	Class	Pos
1988	Production C	51
1988	Junior	38

Dickinson, Barry

Year	Class	Pos
1969	Lightweight 125	20
1970	Lightweight 125	9

Dickinson, Gary

Year	Class	Pos
1963	Lightweight 125	10
1964	Lightweight 125	8
1965	Lightweight 125	12
1966	Lightweight 125	13
1967	Lightweight 125	32
1968	Lightweight 125	8
1969	Lightweight 125	3

Dickinson, Garry

Year	Class	Pos
1988	Production C	60

Diepold, Karlheinz

Year	Class	Pos
1984	Formula 2	27
1984	Production A	10

Dobson, Ken

Year	Class	Pos
1984	Formula 1	19
1984	Production B	5
1985	Formula 1	32
1985	Production 250	11
1986	Production B	17
1986	Production C	15
1986	Senior	25

Donnan, John

Year	Class	Pos
1989	SS600	38
1990	SS600	34
1991	SS600	24
1996	Formula 1	33
1996	Junior	46
1996	Senior	=40
1997	Junior	36
1997	Production	49

Douglas, Chris

Year	Class	Pos
1994	S/car B	41

Duffus, Ian

Year	Class	Pos
1988	Production B	15
1990	Senior	15
1991	Formula 1	10
1992	SS600	10
1993	SS600	8
1995	Junior	1
1996	Formula 1	4
1996	Junior	2
1996	Production	2

Duffy, Frank

Year	Class	Pos
1990	Lightweight 125	7

Dugdale, Alan

Year	Class	Pos
1963	Lightweight 125	16
1987	Production D	=15

Dunn, Mike

Year	Class	Pos
1976	Production 10 lap	23
1994	Lightweight 125	24

Dunlop, Joey

Year	Class	Pos
1981	Formula 1	3
1982	Formula 1	2
1983	Formula 1	1
1983	Senior Classic	3
1984	Formula 1	1
1984	Premier Classic	2
1985	Formula 1	1
1985	Junior	1
1985	Production 750	22
1985	Senior	1
1986	Formula 1	1
1986	Production C	4
1986	Senior	4
1987	Formula 1	1
1987	Junior	8
1987	Production B	18
1987	Senior	1
1988	Production B	5
1988	Production C	11
1988	Formula 1	1
1988	Junior	1
1988	Senior	1
1990	Formula 1	8
1990	Senior	16
1991	Lightweight 125	2
1991	Junior	5
1991	SS600	6
1991	Senior	1
1992	Formula 1	3
1992	Lightweight 125	1
1992	SS600	9
1993	Formula 1	14
1993	Lightweight 125	1
1993	Junior	3
1993	Senior	11
1994	Formula 1	3
1994	Lightweight 125	1
1994	SS600	7
1994	Junior	1
1994	Senior	3
1995	Formula 1	2
1995	Lightweight	1
1995	Junior	4
1995	Senior	1
1996	Formula 1	7
1996	Lightweight	1
1996	Lightweight 125	1
1996	Senior	2
1997	Formula 1	6
1997	Lightweight	1
1997	Lightweight 125	10
1997	Junior	5
1997	Senior	7

Dunlop, Robert

Year	Class	Pos
1985	Production 250	6
1987	Production D	6
1988	Production C	16
1988	Formula 1	13
1988	Senior	12
1989	Formula 1	7
1989	Lightweight 125	1
1989	Senior	4
1990	Lightweight 125	1
1991	Lightweight 125	1
1992	Lightweight 125	2
1993	Lightweight 125	2
1997	Lightweight 125	3

Dunnell, Tony

Year	Class	Pos
1967	Production 500	7

Dunphy, Joe

Year	Class	Pos
1964	Lightweight 125	13

Dynes, Gary

Year	Class	Pos
1993	Junior	15
1993	Senior	34
1994	Junior	10
1996	Lightweight	12
1996	Lightweight 125	6
1996	Senior	21
1997	Lightweight	5
1997	Lightweight 125	7

East, Dave
1994 SS600 33
1995 Junior 26
Ebert, H.
1964 Lightweight 125 16
Eckert, Klaus
1994 SS600 38
Elbon, James
1982 Formula 1 33
1982 Formula 2 24
1983 Formula 2 35
Elridge, Steve
1975 Production 10 lap 44
1976 Production 10 lap 34
English, Glen
1992 Lightweight 125 24
1994 Lightweight 125 5
1994 SS600 42
1995 Lightweight 125 6
1996 Lightweight 17
1996 Lightweight 125 3
1997 Lightweight 125 4
Evans, Brad
1993 SS600 42
Evans, Hugh
1973 Production 750 8
1973 Formula 750 20
1974 Senior 29
1976 Production 10 lap 41
Evans, L. E.
1964 Lightweight 125 22
1964 50cc 13
Evans, R. D.
1964 Lightweight 125 25

Farmer, Gordon
1984 Production C 11
Farmer, Mark
1986 Production B 40
Farmer, Stephen
1991 Junior 28
Faulkner, Chris
1986 Production D 26
Fearns, Tommy
1967 50cc 7
Finch, Frank
1991 SS600 22
1993 SS600 18

1995 Junior 19
1996 Junior 28
1996 Senior 22
Finney, Ken
1964 Lightweight 125 38
1965 Lightweight 250 24
1967 Lightweight 125 24
1968 Lightweight 125 15
Fitzgerald, Terence
1997 Junior 33
Flynn, Gerry
1989 Lightweight 125 28
Flynn, Marc
1994 SS600 10
1995 Formula 1 7
1995 Senior 13
1997 Formula 1 5
Fogarty, Carl
1986 Production C 12
1986 Production D 17
1987 Junior 4
1987 Production D 9
1988 Production C 12
1988 Formula 1 4
1988 Senior 7
1989 Formula 1 4
1989 Production 750 1
1989 Lightweight 125 3
1989 Junior 4
1990 Formula 1 1
1990 SS400 2
1990 Junior 4
1990 Senior 1
1991 Formula 1 2
Foll, Roland
1964 Lightweight 125 10
Foster, Peter
1997 Production 55
Fox, Karl
1988 Production C 35
1994 SS600 59

Gabbott, Steve
1989 Lightweight 125 18
1990 Lightweight 125 25
Gable, Colin
1988 Formula 1 24
1989 Formula 1 10
1990 Formula 1 21

1992 Formula 1 15
1992 Senior 8
1994 Formula 1 9
1994 SS600 22
1994 Senior 11
1995 Junior 3
1996 Junior 4
1996 Production 4
Galbraith, Eric
1983 Formula 2 34
1989 SS600 24
1989 Formula 1 23
1989 Senior 21
Gallagher, Pat
1993 S/car A 15
1993 S/car B 8
Gardiner, Brian
1993 Formula 1 21
1993 SS600 14
1993 Senior 14
1994 Formula 1 12
1994 SS600 14
1994 Senior 13
1995 Junior 13
Garner, Charles
1972 Production 250 9
Gasse, Helmut
1984 Production B 23
Geeson, Les
1965 Lightweight 125 13
1966 Lightweight 125 21
George, Alex
1979 Formula 1 1
1979 Schweppes Cl. 1
1981 Formula 1 6
1981 Classic 3
Geulen, Elmer
1984 Production A 16
Gibbs, Steven
1981 Formula 2 24
Gilmour, Philip
1993 Formula 1 27
1993 Senior 36
1994 Formula 1 30
1994 Senior 39
1996 Junior 53
Glass, Derek
1988 Production C 20
1988 Junior 18

Gleed, Brian
1966 50cc 5
1967 50cc 8
Goodfellow, Dave
1979 Formula 1 16
1979 Formula 2 10
Goodley, Dave
1990 Formula 1 26
1990 Senior 19
1992 Formula 1 22
1992 Senior 14
1994 SS600 20
1997 Production 19
Gordon, Steve
1994 Senior 34
Graham, Alan
1994 Lightweight 125 21
Graham, Stuart
1966 Lightweight 250 2
Graham, Stuart
1988 Production C 58
Granie, Marc
1988 Production C 44
Grant, Mick
1980 Formula 1 1
1980 Classic 2
Gray, Brian
1986 S/car A 11
Greasley, Dick
1974 S/car 2 18
Gregory, Chris
1969 Lightweight 125 19
Grein, Martin
1990 SS600 35
Griffith, David
1988 Production C 21
1988 Junior 25
Griffiths, Les
1965 50cc 6
1966 50cc 7
1967 50cc 5
1968 50cc 3
Griffiths, Jason
1992 Formula 1 10
1993 Formula 1 4
1993 Senior 4
1994 Junior 3
1996 Formula 1 5
1996 Lightweight 3

1996 Junior 5
1996 Senior 7
1997 Lightweight 9
1997 Production 18
1997 Senior 15
Grigor, Graham
1984 Production A 13
Grotefeld, Terry
1966 Lightweight 125 19
Guilhat, Alain
1997 Lightweight 125 36
Gustafsson, Bo
1967 Lightweight 125 9
Gustafson, F.
1964 Lightweight 125 24
Gustafsson, Dan
1997 Junior 49
Gustafsson, Peter
1997 Junior 47
Guy, Chris
1980 Formula 2 2
1980 Classic 9
Guymer, Mike
1988 Formula 1 47
1990 Formula 1 40
1990 Senior 30

Hackett, Ron
1970 Lightweight 125 19
1972 Lightweight 125 5
Haeltert, Jerome van
1992 SS600 34
1993 SS600 37
1994 SS600 60
1995 Junior 42
1995 Senior 45
1996 Junior 58
Hanna, Ray
1992 Lightweight 125 32
Hailwood, Mike
1961 Lightweight 125 1
1961 Lightweight 250 2
1966 Lightweight 125 6
1966 Lightweight 250 1
1966 Senior 1
1967 Lightweight 250 1
1967 Junior 1
1967 Senior 1
Hall, Martin

1984 Production B 11
Hanna, Clifford
1990 Lightweight 125 19
Hanna, Ray
1986 Production D 18
1989 SS600 31
1989 Senior 42
1997 Lightweight 125 17
Harris, Shaun
1995 Lightweight 5
1996 Lightweight 13
Harrison, Kenny
1979 Formula 2 12
1991 Senior 10
Harrison, Rob
1994 SS600 41
Harvey, Phil
1995 Lightweight 125 25
1996 Lightweight 125 12
1997 Lightweight 125 19
Haslam, Neil
1994 Formula 1 36
1994 Formula 1 36
Haslam, Ron
1978 Formula 2 4
1979 Formula 1 3
1980 Formula 3 3
1980 Classic 3
1981 Formula 1 2
1982 Formula 1 1
Haynes, Ray
1992 Junior 24
1993 Junior 35
Hazlett, Steve
1990 Senior 8
Head, Tony
1986 Production B 48
1986 Senior 36
Heath, Bob
1988 Production B 13
1990 Formula 1 18
1990 Junior 9
1990 Senior 21
1991 Lightweight 125 3
1991 Junior 7
1992 Junior 7
1993 Lightweight 125 3
1996 Lightweight 125 5
1997 Lightweight 125 11

Heath, Chris
1996 Junior 32
1996 Production 32
1997 Junior 13
1997 Production 12
1997 Senior 10
Heckles, Keith
1974 Production 250 9
Henderson, Bill
1976 Production 10 lap 4
Henderson, John
1995 Formula 1 25
1996 Junior 42
1996 Senior 23
Henley, Russell
1997 Lightweight 125 21
Henry, Sammy
1987 Junior 14
1989 Junior 16
Henshaw, Steve
1988 Junior 20
1989 Formula 1 18
Hepburn, John
1994 SS600 27
1994 Senior 17
1996 Junior 37
1996 Senior 29
1997 Junior 19
1997 Senior 24
Heppenstall, Peter
1995 Junior 58
Heukerott, Gerhardt
1968 Junior 38
Heys, Joseph
1991 S/car A 21
1991 S/car B 12
Higginson, George
1994 Junior 32
Higham, Jack
1975 Production 10 lap 34
1976 Production 10 lap 10
Hill, Billy
1982 Formula 2 6
Hill, Bob
1980 Formula 3 16
1981 Formula 3 21
Hill, Brian
1990 SS600 24
Hislop, Steve

1988 Production B 1
1988 Production C 3
1988 Senior 2
1989 SS600 1
1989 Formula 1 1
1989 Production 750 3
1989 Senior 1
1990 Formula 1 9
1990 SS400 6
1990 Junior 2
1991 Formula 1 1
1991 SS400 2
1991 SS600 1
1991 Senior 1
1992 SS600 2
1994 Formula 1 1
1994 Senior 1
Hodson, Jim
1988 Production C 39
1988 Senior 55
1989 SS600 20
1991 Lightweight 125 11
1995 Lightweight 125 15
1996 Lightweight 125 18
1997 Junior 16
Holden, Rob
1990 Formula 1 16
1990 Senior 14
Horsham, Phil
1964 50cc 11
Horspole, Garry
1994 S/car A 13
1994 S/car B 17
1997 S/car A 7
1997 S/car B 5
Horton, Clive
1975 Production 10 lap 12
Howarth, Alastair
1997 Production 37
Hudson, John
1964 Lightweight 125 23
1966 Lightweight 125 26
1967 Lightweight 125 19
1968 Lightweight 125 11
1969 Lightweight 250 22
1970 Lightweight 125 13
Huggett, Fred
1981 Formula 1 17
Hughes, David

1975 Production 10 lap 18
Hughes, Gerry
1989 Lightweight 125 24
Hughes, Kevin
1986 Formula 1 33
1986 Production =8
1987 Formula 2 9
Hughes, Tony
1987 Production D 36
1988 Production D 27
Hunt, Mick
1984 Formula 2 25
Hunter, James
1987 Formula 2 40
Hunter, Richard
1978 Formula 3 17
1979 Formula 3 2
Huntingdon, David
1985 Production 750 41
1986 Production B 62
Hurlstone, John
1984 Production B 18
Hurst, Roger
1986 Production B 25
Hutchings, Tony
1964 50cc 14
Huxley, Derek
1979 Formula 3 13
1981 Formula 3 13
1984 Formula 1 12
I'Anson, Rob
1994 SS600 32
1996 Junior 33
Ireland, Dennis
1989 Formula 1 16
1989 Senior 12
Irwin, Peter
1993 Lightweight 125 23
Jackson, Alan
1977 Formula 2 1
1978 Formula 2 1
1979 Formula 2 1
1986 Production C 10
Jackson, Alan Bud
1986 Production C 21
1987 Production D 27
1987 Senior 35

1989 Senior 41
1990 Lightweight 125 5
1991 Lightweight 125 20
1992 Lightweight 125 23
1993 Lightweight 125 9
1994 Lightweight 125 8
1995 Lightweight 125 7
1995 Lightweight 17
1996 Lightweight 20
1996 Lightweight 125 13
1996 Senior 43
Jackson, Bob
1984 Production A 7
1986 Production C 7
1986 Production D 24
1987 Formula 2 14
1988 Production C 14
1988 Junior 14
1989 Formula 1 14
1989 Production 750 7
1989 Senior 11
1990 Formula 1 10
1990 SS600 5
1990 Senior 9
1991 Formula 1 6
1991 Lightweight 125 5
1991 SS600 3
1991 Senior 6
1992 Formula 1 7
1992 Lightweight 125 13
1992 SS600 5
1993 SS600 2
1994 Formula 1 11
1994 SS600 5
1994 Senior 19
1995 Junior 23
1996 Junior 9
1996 Production 24
1997 Junior 6
Jackson, Matthew
1997 Lightweight 125 29
Jackson, Sean
1996 Production 31
Jacques-Jean, Michel
1997 S/car B 39
Jamison, Norman
1990 Lightweight 125 30
Jansson, Sten
1997 Junior 50

Jarmann, Peter
1993 SS600 38
1994 SS600 64
1996 Junior 67
1997 Production 54
Jarmer, Bo
1992 SS600 38
Jarmer, Stig
1992 SS600 26
Jefferies, David
1996 Junior 16
1996 Production 10
1996 Senior 16
Jefferies, Nick
1987 Formula 1 6
1987 Production B 6
1987 Senior 5
1988 Production A 6
1988 Production B 6
1988 Production C 10
1988 Formula 1 2
1991 Formula 1 7
1991 SS400 8
1991 SS600 18
1991 Senior 5
1991 Formula 1 4
1992 SS400 4
1992 SS600 4
1992 Senior 4
1993 Formula 1 1
1993 SS400 6
1993 Junior 6
1993 Senior 2
1994 SS600 6
1995 Formula 1 4
1995 Junior 2
1995 Senior 4
1996 Formula 1 2
1996 Junior 8
1996 Production 7
1996 Senior 3
John, Stephen
1997 Lightweight 125 35
Johnson, Eddie
1963 Lightweight 125 12
1965 Lightweight 125 15
1967 Lightweight 125 14
Johnson, Geoff
1985 Production 1500 1

1986 Formula 1 2
1986 Production B =8
1986 Senior 2
Johnson, Steve
1987 Formula 2 21
1989 SS600 17
1992 Lightweight 125 5
Jones, Frank
1980 Formula 2 24
Jones, Ian
1988 Production D 19
Junk, Courtney
1976 Production 10 lap 38
Kaletsch, Dirk
1994 Lightweight 125 22
1995 Lightweight 125 27
1996 Lightweight 125 27
1997 Lightweight 125 32
Kaye, Brian
1965 Lightweight 125 31
1966 Lightweight 125 30
1967 Lightweight 125 22
1968 Lightweight 125 18
1969 Lightweight 125 23
1970 Lightweight 125 22
Kaye, T.
1992 Lightweight 125 25
Kehrer, Johannes
1992 SS600 36
1993 Junior 26
1994 Formula 1 42
1994 Junior 21
1996 Lightweight 32
1996 Production 39
Kelly, Brian
1997 S/car B 29
Kelly, Derek
1995 Junior 29
1995 Senior 32
1996 Junior 27
1996 Senior 27
1997 Junior 21
Kelly, Neil
1975 Production 10 lap 14
Kerby, Dave
1978 Formula 2 10
1979 Formula 2 15
1980 Formula 2 21

1981 Formula 2 15
1985 Formula 1 57
1985 Formula 2 30
1986 Formula 2 36
1989 SS600 41
Kerner, Hartley
1978 Formula 2 11
1983 Formula 1 19
1983 Senior Classic 33
1984 Formula 2 15
1984 Production B 4
Kettle, Brian
1965 50cc 8
1966 50cc 10
Keys, Trevor
1990 Lightweight 125 29
Kiddie, John
1965 Lightweight 125 25
1966 Lightweight 125 25
1967 Lightweight 125 11
1968 Lightweight 125 7
1969 Lightweight 125 5
1970 Lightweight 125 8
1971 Lightweight 125 3
1972 Production 250 8
1973 Production 250 8
1973 Junior 31
1973 Lightweight 250 35
1973 Lightweight 250 10
1974 Production 250 5
1974 Junior 40
1984 Classic Historic 350 10
Kidson, John
1973 Production 250 10
1975 Production 10 lap 24
1976 Production 10 lap 4
1977 Formula 3 1
King, Ian
1993 SS400 9
1993 SS600 12
1993 Senior 19
Kinsella, Andy
1995 S/car A 49
1996 S/car A 40
1996 S/car B 41
1997 S/car A 34
1997 S/car B 36
Kirk, Ivan
1990 Lightweight 125 23

1991 Lightweight 125 25
1993 Lightweight 125 10
1994 Lightweight 125 10
1995 Lightweight 125 12
Kirkby, John
1978 Formula 2 7
Kirwan, Mal
1977 Formula 3 6
1978 Formula 2 12
1981 Formula 3 18
Kitano, Moto
1960 Lightweight 125 19
1960 Lightweight 250 5
Kleimaier, Bert
1969 Lightweight 125 21
Kneen, Mike
1981 Formula 2 9
Kneen, Phil
1992 SS600 33
1995 Senior 39
1996 Formula 1 35
1996 Senior 39
Knight, Peter
1995 S/car A 22
1995 S/car B 22
1995 S/car A 18
1996 S/car B 15
Knight, Ray
1977 Formula 1 13
1978 Formula 1 13
1979 Formula 1 22
1979 Formula 2 8
1981 Formula 2 17
1983 Formula 1 18
1983 Senior Classic 22
1987 Formula 2 29
1988 Production C 25
1988 Junior 27
1989 SS600 26
1989 Senior 37
1990 SS400 20
1990 SS600 23
1991 SS600 25
1992 SS600 22
1993 SS600 25
1994 SS600 34
Knight, Tom
1992 Formula 1 11
1992 Senior 13

Kohrer, Johannes
1992 Junior 25
Kotnik, Carlos
1990 Formula 1 36
1990 Senior 31
Koyama, Taka
1996 Lightweight 41
1996 Lightweight 125 17

Lattimer, Jeffrey
1997 Senior 36
Law, Ashley
1993 SS600 26
1994 SS600 25
1994 Senior 29
1995 Junior 30
1995 Senior 25
1996 Junior 24
1996 Senior 25
1997 Lightweight 11
1997 Production 20
Lawley, John
1962 50cc 21
1967 50cc 10
1968 50cc 7
1973 Lightweight 125 24
1974 Lightweight 125 24
1975 Lightweight 250 45
Lawley, Stan
1966 50cc 13
1967 50cc 6
Laycock, Eddie
1988 Senior 8
1989 Senior 5
1990 Senior 7
Leach, Dave
1986 Formula 1 29
1986 Formula 2 22
1986 Production B 5
1988 Production C 4
Lee, Gavin
1996 Lightweight 125 2
1997 Lightweight 125 6
Leech, Tim
1994 SS600 35
1995 Senior 30
1996 Junior 25
1997 Junior 29
Leigh, George

1964	Lightweight 125	18	1985	Formula 1	55	1996	Production	1	
1967	Production 250	12	1989	Lightweight 125	2	1996	Senior	1	
Lennon, Reg			1992	Lightweight 125	7	1997	Formula 1	1	
1989	Lightweight 125	11	1994	Junior	5	1997	Junior	2	
1990	Lightweight 125	11	1995	Junior	10	1997	Production	1	
1991	Lightweight 125	23	1995	Senior	18	1997	Senior	1	
1992	Lightweight 125	27	1996	Junior	11	**McCauley, Aubrey**			
1995	Lightweight 125	24	1997	Lightweight	2	1990	Lightweight 125	6	
1996	Lightweight 125	25	1997	Lightweight 125	1	1992	Lightweight 125	22	
1997	Lightweight 125	31	1997	Production	31	1993	Lightweight 125	22	
Linden, Peter			**Loughridge, Tom**			1997	Lightweight 125	14	
1984	Formula 1	16	1970	Lightweight 125	11	**McClements, Sam**			
1984	Senior	12	**Lucas, Malcolm**			1980	Formula 1	3	
1984	Premier Classic	21	1980	Formula 2	3	1980	Classic	6	
1984	Production A	3	1984	Formula 1	11	1988	Senior	10	
1985	Production 1500	5	1984	Production B	8	1989	SS600	30	
1985	Senior	9	**Lunn, Doug**			1989	Formula 1	9	
Linham, Gary			1972	Production 750	8	1989	Senior	7	
1997	Production	28				**McCrea, Kevin**			
Linton, Mark			**McAllister, Ronnie**			1994	SS600	67	
1991	Lightweight 125	28	1997	Junior	45	**McCullough, Denis**			
Livingston, Mark			**McCallen, Phillip**			1992	Lightweight 125	6	
1994	Formula 1	32	1989	SS600	28	1993	Lightweight 125	4	
1994	SS600	37	1989	Formula 1	15	1994	Lightweight 125	2	
1994	Senior	30	1989	Production 750	15	1995	Lightweight 125	4	
1996	Formula 1	23	1989	Lightweight 125	7	1995	Lightweight	6	
Lloyd, Derek			1989	Senior	17	1996	Lightweight	6	
1968	Lightweight 250	13	1990	Formula 1	39	1996	Junior	17	
1993	Formula 1	32	1990	Junior	6	1996	Production	30	
1993	Senior	45	1990	SS600	14	1997	Lightweight 125	2	
1995	Formula 1	21	1991	Formula 1	4	1997	Junior	20	
1996	Senior	26	1991	Lightweight 125	4	**McCullough, John**			
1997	Formula 1	20	1991	Junior	2	1990	Lightweight 125	26	
1997	Senior	17	1991	SS600	5	1991	Lightweight 125	14	
Lock, Brian			1991	Senior	3	**McDonald, Allan**			
1968	50cc	4	1992	Formula 1	1	1990	Formula 1	19	
Lofthouse, Mick			1992	SS400	2	1990	Senior	18	
1992	Lightweight 125	3	1992	SS600	1	1991	Formula 1	11	
Loicht, Martin			1993	Formula 1	2	1991	Senior	13	
1992	Lightweight 125	31	1993	SS600	7	1992	Formula 1	18	
1993	Lightweight 125	14	1993	Senior	1	1992	Senior	16	
1994	Lightweight 125	15	1994	Formula 1	2	1993	Formula 1	19	
1994	SS600	56	1994	SS600	4	1997	Formula 1	17	
1995	Lightweight 125	17	1994	Senior	2	1997	Production	40	
1995	Junior	39	1995	Formula 1	1	1997	Senior	28	
1995	Senior	47	1995	Lightweight	4	**McFarland, Adrian**			
Long, Gary			1996	Formula 1	1	1997	Junior	14	
1995	Junior	22	1996	Lightweight	4	1997	Senior	16	
Lougher, Ian			1996	Junior	1	**McGahan, Chris**			

1995	Lightweight 125	22	1991	SS400	13
1996	Lightweight 125	10	1991	Senior	16
1997	Production	48	1992	Formula 1	23
McGarrity, Mick			1992	SS400	17
1984	Production C	10	1992	Senior	17
1985	Junior	7	1993	Formula 1	33
1985	Production 250	4	1993	SS400	12
1989	Lightweight 125	5	1993	Senior	18
McGladdery, Andy			1994	Formula 1	21
1989	Formula 1	8	1994	SS600	47
1989	Senior	6	1994	SS400	14
McGregor, Graeme			1994	Senior	22
1989	Formula 1	5	1995	Formula 1	14
1989	Senior	3	1995	Senior	19
1990	Formula 1	7	1996	Formula 1	14
1990	Senior	13	1996	Lightweight	34
McGuiness, John			1996	Senior	11
1996	Lightweight	15	1997	Lightweight	30
1997	Junior	24	1997	Junior	18
McGurk, Tony			1997	Production	43
1974	Production 500	9	1997	Senior	23
McHenry, Eamon			**Maeda, Jun**		
1974	Lightweight 125	20	1997	Senior	41
McKane, Terry			**Marcusson, Peter**		
1975	Production 10 lap	25	1993	Junior	19
1976	Production 10 lap	25	1993	SS600	31
1977	Formula 2	6	**Marshall, Roger**		
McLean, Craig			1983	Formula 1	4
1993	SS600	33	1984	Formula 1	2
1993	Senior	39	1984	Senior	2
1994	Formula 1	24	1985	Senior	2
1994	SS600	24	1986	Senior	6
1994	Senior	32	**Martin, Paddy**		
1995	Junior	33	1988	Production C	54
McMillan, Ricky			**Mason, Dave**		
1987	Senior	42	1978	Formula 2	3
McMillan, Dennis			1979	Formula 1	24
1975	Production 10 lap	18	1981	Formula 2	6
McMullan, Geoff			1982	Formula 3	4
1995	Lightweight	39	1983	Formula 2	33
McNally, Owen			**Mason, Steve**		
1997	Lightweight 125	5	1989	Lightweight 125	12
Madsen-Mygdal, Dave			**Mast, Christopher**		
1988	Production B	48	1995	Junior	45
1988	Formula 1	41	**Mates, Charlie**		
1989	Formula 1	35	1965	Lightweight 125	19
1989	Production 750	23	1965	50cc	4
1990	Formula 1	30	**Mawdsley, Kevin**		
1990	Senior	20	1986	Production D	8

Year	Class	Pos
1988	Production C	7
1988	Junior	11
1988	Senior	26
Meinhardt, Peter		
1997	Formula 1	30
Mellor, Ron		
1975	Production 10 lap	28
Middleton, Jeffrey		
1978	Formula 3	8
1979	Formula 3	11
Milton, Rob		
1986	Production C	14
Minter, Derek		
1962	Lightweight 125	4
1962	Lightweight 250	1
1962	50cc	9
Moffitt, Dave		
1990	Lightweight 125	21
Montano, Thomas		
1993	SS600	20
1994	Formula 1	25
1994	SS600	23
1994	Senior	35
1996	Formula 1	21
1996	Junior	23
1996	Senior	15
1997	Junior	10
Moodie, Jim		
1988	Production C	37
1990	SS400	9
1990	SS600	6
1993	Formula 1	6
1993	Junior	2
1993	SS600	1
1996	Lightweight	2
1996	Junior	7
1997	Senior	2
Moore, Bruce		
1996	S/car A	42
1997	S/car A	17
Morris, Dave		
1990	Formula 1	22
1990	Senior	7
1991	Formula 1	15
1991	Senior	15
1992	Formula 1	19
1997	Lightweight	15
Morris, Ian		
1990	Formula 1	17
1990	Senior	23
1991	Formula 1	13
1991	Senior	8
Morrison, Brian		
1988	Production A	13
1988	Production B	2
1988	Production C	1
1988	Formula 1	7
1988	Junior	4
1988	Senior	6
1989	SS600	5
1989	Formula 1	2
1989	Production 750	5
1990	Formula 1	4
1990	Senior	5
Mortimer, Charles		
1984	Production C	14
Mortimer, Richard		
1990	Lightweight 125	9
1991	Lightweight 125	17
1992	Lightweight 125	15
1994	Lightweight 125	16
1995	Lightweight 125	28
1996	Lightweight 125	11
Morscher, Gerhard		
1988	Production C	55
1990	Lightweight 125	17
1991	Lightweight 125	22
1992	Lightweight 125	30
Moynihan, Steve		
1976	Production 10 lap	12
1986	Production D	16
1987	Production D	25
Muir, Peter		
1987	Formula 2	24
Murden, Rupert		
1991	Lightweight 125	32
Murdoch, Stuart		
1997	Junior	42
Murphy, Kevin		
1997	Formula 1	36
Murray, Bernard		
1975	Production 10 lap	19
1976	Production 10 lap	28
Murray, Kenneth		
1992	Lightweight 125	19
Murray, Steve		
1964	Lightweight 125	19
1965	Lightweight 125	17
1966	Lightweight 125	17
1968	Lightweight 125	6
1969	Lightweight 125	4
1970	Lightweight 125	4
1976	Production 10 lap	12
1984	Production C	19
1986	Production D	31
1992	Lightweight 125	34
1994	Lightweight 125	23
Musson, David		
1981	Classic	22
Musson, John		
1978	Formula 3	14
Nation, Trevor		
1984	Production B	1
Newton, Ian		
1989	Lightweight 125	4
1990	Lightweight 125	2
Newton, Joseph		
1995	S/car A	41
1996	S/car B	40
Nicholls, Keith		
1988	Production C	48
1988	Junior	35
Nicholls, Paul		
1995	Junior	32
Nicholls, Phil		
1984	Production B	27
1985	Production 250	5
1986	Production D	15
1986	Production C	5
1987	Production D	7
1988	Production C	15
1989	SS600	13
1989	Formula 1	22
1989	Production 750	=11
1989	Senior	13
1992	Lightweight 125	21
1993	SS400	10
1994	Formula 1	29
1994	SS400	8
1996	Junior	38
Nightingale, John		
1982	Formula 2	29
1983	Formula 2	38
1985	Formula 1	59
1984	Formula 2	35
1986	Formula 2	48
1987	Formula 2	41
Nobbs, David		
1989	Lightweight 125	8
1990	Lightweight 125	12
1991	Lightweight 125	21
1992	Lightweight 125	33
1993	Lightweight 125	17
1994	Lightweight 125	18
1995	Lightweight 125	20
1996	Lightweight 125	22
1997	Lightweight 125	33
Noblett, Mick		
1992	Formula 1	21
1992	Senior	18
1995	Junior	34
1995	Senior	38
Nonoo, Yuszuf		
1988	Production 750	31
Noon, Stuart		
1981	Formula 2	20
1982	Formula 2	17
1986	Formula 2	42
Noone, Justin		
1989	Production 750	26
Nusmuller, Gunther		
1979	Formula 2	11
1981	Formula 1	27
Nuttall, Peter		
1992	S/car A	10
1992	S/car B	23
1993	S/car A	9
1993	S/car B	23
O'Connor, Michael		
1991	Lightweight 125	12
1992	Lightweight 125	12
O'Leary, David		
1988	Production	46
1993	Formula 1	20
1993	Junior	20
1993	Senior	26
O'Neill, Brian		
1973	Lightweight 125	20
1974	Lightweight 125	23
Odlin, Phil		
1979	Formula 2	7
1980	Formula 2	4
1981	Senior	26
1981	Formula 2	2
Orritt, Paul		
1996	Junior	44
1997	Junior	31
1997	Production	47
O'Sullivan, Joseph		
1993	SS600	46
1994	SS600	66
1994	Lightweight	42
1996	Junior	65
1997	Lightweight	50
Oxley, Mat		
1985	Production 250	1
Padgett, Gary		
1985	Junior	15
1985	Production 250	3
Palmer, Chris		
1990	Lightweight 125	13
Parrish, Steve		
1975	Production 10 lap	11
Parrott, Richard		
1993	Lightweight 125	6
Patrignani, Roberto		
1989	Production 750	33
Pearson, John		
1965	Lightweight 125	40
Penny Graham		
1967	Production 500	4
1969	Production 500	1
1970	Senior	41
1971	Production 500	2
1971	Formula 750	12
1972	Production 500	6
1972	Senior	24
Petty, Chris		
1987	Formula 2	36
1988	Production C	43
1988	Junior	33
1989	SS600	26
1993	Formula 1	29
1993	Senior	30
1994	SS600	43
1995	Junior	37
1996	Junior	30
1997	Junior	37
1997	Senior	32
Phillis, Tom		
1960	Lightweight 125	10
1961	Lightweight 125	3

1961 Lightweight 250   2
1962 Lightweight 125   3
1962 Lightweight 250   3

Piercy, Nigel
1995 Lightweight 125   16
1996 Junior   21
1996 Senior   18
1997 Production   39

Pink, Jim
1965 50cc.   7
1966 50cc   8
1968 50cc   5

Pither, Dave
1986 Senior   30

Pitsch, G.
1965 Lightweight 125   39

Plenderleith, George
1963 Lightweight 250   13
1964 Lightweight 125   17
1965 Lightweight 250   16
1966 Lightweight 125   16
1966 Lightweight 250   9
1968 Lightweight 125   9
1969 Junior   35
1970 Lightweight 125   17

Plumridge, Ian
1963 50cc   6
1964 50cc   10

Poole, Loren
1994 SS600   15

Porter, Colin
1975 Production 10 lap   53
1977 Formula 1   19
1977 Jubilee   39

Porter, Harvey
1975 Production 10 lap   34

Porter, Lindsay
1971 Lightweight 125   8
1972 Lightweight 125   4
1973 Lightweight 125   6
1974 Lightweight 125   17

Potts, John
1995 S/car A   48
1995 S/car B   36
1996 S/car A   29
1996 S/car B   26
1997 S/car A   28
1997 S/car B   40

Power, Jonathan

1994 SS600   50

Powell, Andrew
1995 Junior   40
1995 Senior   42

Poxon, Mick
1978 Formula 3   4
1980 Formula 3   10

Pritchard, Cliff
1997 S/car A   36
1997 S/car B   33

Pullan, Lee
1991 Lightweight 125   15
1992 Lightweight 125   11
1995 Junior   9
1995 Senior   15
1996 Junior   10

Quayle, Richard
1997 Production   22

Radcliffe, Gary
1988 Formula 1   23
1988 Senior   32
1990 Formula 1   15
1990 Senior   12
1991 Senior   9
1992 Formula 1   14
1992 Senior   11
1993 Formula 1   10
1993 Senior   9
1994 Formula 1   4
1994 Junior   11
1994 Senior   6
1995 Formula 1   10
1995 Senior   12

Rae, Bill
1987 Formula 2   30

Randall, Doug
1976 Classic 1000   30
1977 Formula 1   26
1977 Classic   27
1981 Formula 3   14

Randla, Juri
1990 Formula 1   47

Raudsik, Juri
1990 Formula 1   48

Raybould, John
1982 Formula 1   26
1991 Formula 1   24

Rea, Johnny
1989 SS600   10
1990 Senior   11
1991 Formula 1   12
1991 Senior   12
1992 Senior   10

Rea, Stanley
1992 Lightweight 125   4
1996 Lightweight 125   8
1997 Lightweight   14

Read, Phil
1977 Formula 1   1
1978 Schweppes Cl.   4

Rechberger, Toni
1992 SS600   21
1994 SS600   54

Redfern, Fran
1968 50cc   10

Redman, Jim
1961 Lightweight 125   4
1961 Lightweight 250   3
1962 Lightweight 125   5
1962 Lightweight 250   2
1963 Lightweight 125   6
1963 Lightweight 250   1
1963 Junior   1
1964 Lightweight 125   2
1964 Lightweight 250   1
1964 Junior   1
1965 Lightweight 250   1
1965 Junior   1

Revett, Chris
1974 Production 500   7
1975 Production 10 lap   11

Reynolds, Hugh
1997 Junior   27
1997 Senior   37

Richards, Brian
1964 Lightweight 125   14
1965 Lightweight 125   32
1966 Lightweight 125   15

Richard, Brian
1986 Junior   24

Richards, Ian
1977 Formula 1   3
1979 Formula 2   4

Richardson, Chris
1997 Lightweight 125   9

Richardson, Melvin

1989 Lightweight 125   25
1990 Lightweight 125   32
1991 Lightweight 125   29

Richardson, Neil
1997 Lightweight   10
1997 Lightweight 125   16

Richardson, Steve
1996 Junior   57
1997 Formula 1   21
1997 Senior   34

Ritchie, Trevor
1989 Lightweight 125   16
1990 Lightweight 125   18
1995 Lightweight 125   9
1996 Lightweight 125   15
1997 Lightweight 125   18

Robb, Tommy
1962 Lightweight 125   2
1962 50cc   3
1963 Lightweight 125   7
1963 Lightweight 250   5
1971 Production 250   3
1973 Production 250   3

Roberts, Eddie
1975 Production 10 lap   8
1976 Production 10 lap   28

Robertson, Bill
1983 Formula 2   21

Robertson, Bill
1989 Lightweight 125   20

Robinson, Allan
1966 50cc   12

Robinson, Graham
1968 Production 500   5

Robinson, Jackie
1972 Lightweight 125   14

Robinson, Mark
1995 Junior   50
1996 Junior   59

Robinson, Mick
1988 Production C   32

Rodgers, Jimmy
1990 Lightweight 125   27
1991 Lightweight 125   26
1992 Lightweight 125   29
1993 Lightweight 125   12
1994 Lightweight 125   18
1995 Lightweight 125   13
1996 Lightweight 125   =19

1997 Lightweight 125   24

Roebuck, Ted
1991 Lightweight 125   18
1992 Lightweight 125   17
1993 Lightweight 125   11
1997 Lightweight 125   25

Roebury, Ron
1982 Formula 2   18
1982 Classic   32
1983 Formula 2   16
1983 Senior Classic   36
1984 Classic Historic 350   6
1984 Production B   25
1985 Formula 2   29

Rogers, Jimmy
1989 Lightweight 125   23

Rogers, Paul
1976 S/car 1000   22

Ross, Andrew
1988 Production C   49
1988 Junior   31

Rowe, Les
1989 Lightweight 125   22

Rowe, R. E.
1961 Lightweight 125   22

Rubatto, Peter
1984 Formula 1   4
1985 Formula 2   18

Rutter, Frank
1975 Production 10 lap   22
1980 Formula 1   31
1981 Formula 1   10
1982 Formula 1   10
1984 Formula 1   18
1984 Production B   7
1989 SS600   33

Rutter, Michael
1994 Formula 1   17
1995 Junior   18
1996 Junior   31
1996 Production   22
1997 Formula 1   2
1997 Junior   3
1997 Production   9

Rutter, Tony
1975 Production 10 lap   19
1979 Formula 3   4
1987 Formula 2   32
1988 Production C   45

| 1988 | Junior | 37 |

Ryan, Brandan
| 1980 | Formula 2 | 17 |

Ryder, Don
| 1971 | Lightweight 125 | 16 |
| 1973 | Lightweight 125 | 25 |

Salle, Mark
| 1984 | Formula 1 | 17 |
| 1984 | Production B | 6 |

Sawyer, Geoff
1994	SS400	20
1995	Formula 1	30
1995	Lightweight	26
1995	Senior	40
1996	Lightweight	37
1996	Production	43
1996	Senior	45

Scheimann, Walter
| 1963 | Lightweight 125 | 14 |
| 1965 | Lightweight 125 | 5 |

Scully, Barry
| 1975 | Production 10 lap | 14 |

Seward, Michael
1987	Formula 2	7
1988	Production C	9
1988	Junior	8
1989	SS600	22

Shand, Alan
1991	S/car A	15
1991	S/car B	14
1992	S/car A	30
1994	S/car A	15
1994	S/car B	19

Shields, Dave
| 1988 | Lightweight 125 | 10 |
| 1990 | Lightweight 125 | 22 |

Shimazaki, Sadao
1960	Lightweight 125	8
1961	Lightweight 125	5
1962	50cc	10

Shimmin, Danny
| 1994 | SS400 | 16 |
| 1995 | Junior | 46 |

Simmonds, Dave
| 1966 | Junior | 8 |
| 1966 | 50cc | 6 |

Simmons, Roy
| 1973 | Production 250 | 13 |

| 1990 | SS400 | 22 |
| 1991 | SS400 | 26 |

Simpson, Ian
1993	Junior	4
1994	Junior	4
1996	Junior	3
1996	Production	12
1996	Senior	10
1997	Formula 1	4
1997	Lightweight	7
1997	Junior	1
1997	Senior	3

Skold, Peter
| 1985 | Production 1500 | 15 |

Smart, F.
| 1971 | Lightweight 125 | 7 |

Smith, Bill
1963	Lightweight 250	3
1964	Lightweight 125	7
1966	Lightweight 125	18
1968	Junior	3
1971	Junior	3
1971	Production 250	1
1972	Junior	16
1973	Production 500	1
1978	Formula 3	1
1979	Formula 3	7
1982	Formula 1	9
1984	Production A	15
1988	Production B	47

Smith, David
1990	Lightweight 125	16
1991	Lightweight 125	30
1992	Lightweight 125	36

Smith, Richard
1993	SS600	17
1994	Formula 1	27
1994	SS600	27
1994	Senior	15

Smith, Roger
| 1994 | SS600 | 68 |

Smith, Simon
1993	SS600	22
1994	SS600	19
1994	Senior	24
1996	Production	19
1997	Junior	12
1997	Production	15
1997	Senior	14

Smyth, Brian
| 1993 | SS600 | 29 |
| 1995 | Senior | 41 |

Soothill, Darren
| 1997 | Production | 23 |

Spargo, Nathan
| 1997 | Formula 1 | 28 |
| 1997 | Production | 45 |

Steele, Trevor
| 1976 | Production 10 lap | 38 |

Stengl, Manfred
1984	Production A	17
1990	SS400	24
1991	SS400	27

Stephens, John
1976	Production 10 lap	23
1978	Formula 3	3
1979	Formula 1	27
1979	Formula 3	12
1980	Formula 1	12
1980	Formula 3	9
1981	Formula 3	8
1982	Formula 1	28

Stevens, Fred
| 1961 | Lightweight 250 | 13 |
| 1966 | Lightweight 125 | 14 |

Stevenson, Gary
1990	Lightweight 125	14
1991	Lightweight 125	19
1994	Lightweight 125	25

Stirner, Michael
1992	SS400	29
1992	SS600	39
1993	SS600	45
1997	Junior	51
1997	Production	59

Storey, Ron
| 1982 | Formula 1 | 35 |

Suzuki, Giichi
| 1959 | Lightweight 125 | 7 |
| 1960 | Lightweight 125 | 7 |

Suzuki, Junzo
| 1959 | Lightweight 125 | 11 |

Swallow, Richard
| 1989 | Lightweight 125 | 6 |
| 1989 | Junior | 9 |

Swann, Ray
| 1987 | Formula 2 | 12 |

Takahashi, Kunimitsu
| 1961 | Lightweight 250 | 4 |
| 1963 | Lightweight 125 | 8 |

Talton, Robert
1987	Formula 2	28
1988	Production C	26
1988	Junior	15

Tanaka, Teisuke
1959	Lightweight 125	8
1960	Lightweight 125	9
1960	Lightweight 250	6

Taniguchi, Naomi
1959	Lightweight 125	6
1960	Lightweight 125	6
1961	Lightweight 125	8
1961	Lightweight 250	5
1964	50cc	6

Tansley, Roy
| 1996 | S/car A | 31 |
| 1996 | S/car B | 33 |

Tapken, Dick
| 1977 | S/car - 2nd leg | 20 |

Taveri, Luigi
1961	Lightweight 125	2
1962	Lightweight 125	1
1962	50cc	2
1963	Lightweight 125	4
1964	Lightweight 125	1
1965	Lightweight 125	2
1965	50cc	1
1966	Lightweight 125	8
1966	50cc	2

Thrush, Gary
1989	Formula 1	41
1989	Production 750	=11
1989	Junior	15
1990	Junior	20

Tomlinson, Bill
| 1971 | Lightweight 125 | 12 |

Tompsett, J.
| 1964 | 50cc | 12 |

Tonkin, Steve
| 1979 | Formula 2 | 3 |

Topping, Michael
1988	SS600	32
1989	Lightweight 125	15
1990	Lightweight 125	3
1991	Lightweight 125	7

Townsend, Keith

| 1996 | Production | 17 |

Trollope, Dennis
1966	Lightweight 125	32
1967	50cc	12
1967	Lightweight 125	16
1967	Lightweight 250	28
1968	Lightweight 125	17
1968	Lightweight 250	31
1989	Lightweight 125	17
1990	Lightweight 125	24
1991	Lightweight 125	31
1992	Lightweight 125	35
1993	Lightweight 125	21

Trubshaw, Keith
| 1976 | Production 10 lap | 10 |

Tunstall, Geoff
| 1984 | Formula 2 | 32 |

Tuxworth, Neil
1974	Production 500	4
1975	Production 10 lap	12
1977	Formula 2	2
1978	Formula 1	27
1978	Formula 2	3
1979	Formula 1	25
1979	Formula 3	6
1989	Senior	32

Tyrell, Mark
| 1996 | Lightweight 125 | 23 |

Udall, Robin
1967	50cc	11
1968	50cc	6
1969	Lightweight 125	25

Vandelbo, Jorgen
| 1993 | Junior | 27 |
| 1994 | Junior | 22 |

Venables, Brian
| 1995 | Formula 1 | 15 |

Verity, Nigel
| 1988 | Production C | 42 |

Vielgut, Karl Heinz
| 1993 | SS600 | 47 |

Vincent, Chris
| 1964 | Lightweight 125 | 12 |

Vine, Rob
| 1984 | Formula 2 | 39 |

Vinsenzi, Graham
| 1964 | Lightweight 125 | 11 |